Susanna's Cookery Book

A Culinary Adventure in Staffordshire

based on the recipe book of

Mrs Susanna Ingleby of Basford Hall

1831-1891

Marion Aldis and Pam Inder

ACKNOWLEDGMENTS

Our most grateful thanks to present members of the Sneyd family who have been unstintingly generous in their encouragement and in giving us access to private family papers, photographs, account books and personal items that once belonged to Susanna. Also to Keele University Library staff for making access to the Sneyd Archive in their Special Collections Library available to us when we needed it.

Our especial thanks go to all the wonderful people of Staffordshire who have contributed invaluably to this book by testing and tasting Susanna's recipes enthusiastically. We also thank those who have delved into their memories and brought to life a bygone era with their vivid descriptions of life and food when they were young. It has been a joy to meet them all.

Finally we thank Susanna for keeping her original recipe book and giving us the opportunity to become part, if only for a while, of her Staffordshire life.

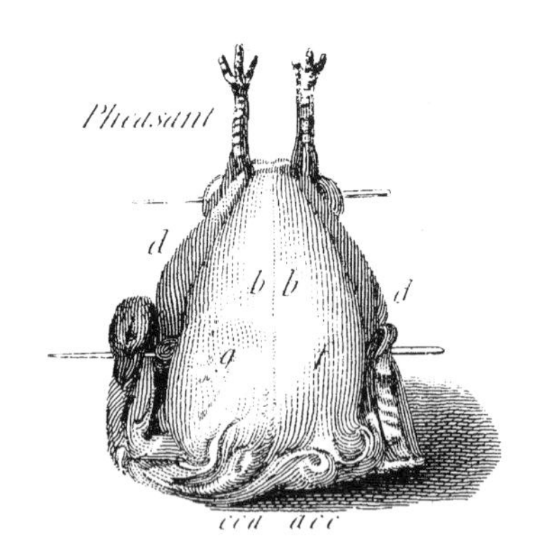

CHURNET VALLEY BOOKS
6 Stanley Street, Leek, Staffordshire. ST13 5HG 01538 399033
thebookshopleek.co.uk

ISBN 1 897949 99 5

Printed by Impress Print

CONTENTS

Salad Dressing.

Boil 4 eggs quite hard, take the yolks, & beat them up with a silver fork quite fine, put a teaspoonful of mixed mustard, a little pepper & a tablespoonful of Salad oil, add by degrees some good cream to the consistency of thick custard, a little salt, & 3 tablespoonsful of good vinegar, last of all beat up well together, & put in a bottle & hand it round with the Salad which must be nicely washed, & cut up.
M.S.

Cure for consumption or bad cough.

Gently boil in a stewpan a pound of good Honey clean scrape, & grate two large sticks of Horseradish stir it into the Honey, let it boil about five minutes but it must be kept continually stirred, Two or three table-spoonfuls a day according to the strength of the patient some time persisted in may

A page of Susanna's Recipe Book

INTRODUCTION

One drowsy afternoon, a couple of years ago in the late 1990s, we were working in the Special Collections Section of Keele University library on the huge archive of Sneyd family papers that are kept there when we stumbled across a recipe book which once belonged to Susanna Ingleby (nee Sneyd). We had not been looking for it - it was given to us by mistake instead of another document we had asked for - but we were fascinated.

By this time we knew a great deal about Susanna and her family; we had already written books about the diaries of her father, the Reverend John Sneyd, and one of her brother's, John William Sneyd, and we were gathering material to write a book about her life. Of all the family, her story, and its discovery, had fascinated us most of all.

In many ways her life had been completely different to ours in the 20th century, and it had been a sad and challenging one. Yet some things were familiar and we certainly could empathise with many of her family problems. Suddenly, finding her cookery book gave us a new and very personal glimpse of her life and her friends. We felt we were getting closer to her as a woman - we too had kept recipe books with well tried and tested recipes given by friends; we too had noted their names beside the recipes.

Like many women of her class Susanna was very well-organised and kept meticulous records of her household expenses, her personal expenses and her gifts to charity; and she kept a detailed recipe book.

Such household records were expected from women of her class and to do them well was an accomplishment. She collected and swapped recipes with her family and friends, and culled them from women's magazines, often noting the page number of the magazine or name of the person who gave her the recipe. Men in her family also contributed recipes for medicines - but none for things to eat.

Quinine Mixture

Sulphate Quinine 20 grains into a bottle holding ½ a pt.
drop on it 60 drops diluted Sulphuric Acid, after well absorbed
fill the bottle with water - A Tablespoonful twice a day
in a wine glass of water -
C.A.S.

Recipes from Susanna's book that we have tested

*These recipes we thought well worth trying

Cakes and biscuits

Puddings and Desserts

Meat Dishes

Vegetarian Dishes

Soups and drinks

Recipes given in the book but not tried

Lobby
Marrow and Ginger Jam
Poor Man's Goose
Pobs
Roast Tongue and Udder

Some of Susanna's recipes are delicious and we have indicated with an asterisk those that have been warmly greeted by the people who cooked or tasted them. A few proved less suited to present day tastes!

Various groups of Staffordshire ladies have been our culinary experts. We have called on many Staffordshire ladies and children who live in the same villages - even the same houses - where Susanna once lived, or who have some connection with her, to test recipes and comment on them.

We are delighted, as we are sure she would have been, that some of the descendants of the Sneyd family have also taken part.

We have also included the memories of food, and shopping, that elderly people living where Susanna lived have shared with us - they conjure up an era not so very far removed from Susanna's. Staffordshire oatcakes, just as she knew them, are still sold and enjoyed throughout North Staffordshire today. But the towns and villages are now very different. If Susanna were to return she would be amazed at how small Ipstones now seems - and amazed to see how much Cheddleton has grown. The shops too have changed out of all recognition. Shoe shops were, in her day, the most numerous type of shop. Cheddleton, for example, with a population of only 370 in 1871, had no less than four. With most people travelling everywhere on foot, over un-metalled roads which were often mud tracks, cobblers were always busy. Even small hamlets were likely to have one. We have included historical information about the villages and towns as we come to them.

Since we know that Susanna was a very economical housekeeper we asked our recipe testers to cook as cheaply as possible and to follow the recipes and ingredients closely, and, as Susanna often recorded the name of the person who had originally given her the recipe so we have put the name of the person who tested it and, where possible, their photograph, in this book. We are most grateful to everyone for their participation and all the work they have put in. Sometimes the instructions that Susanna has written are very scant and in these cases we have added directions from contemporary Victorian cookery books that we know she owned.

You will have realised by now that this is not just a cookery book - although the recipes are all real and tried and tested - but also a history of Victorian day to day life. We have arranged the book in what may seem an unusual way to follow the path that Susanna's life took, starting with Basford Hall where she was born. We will tell you her story as it unfolds through the places where she lived. We hope that you will want to try some of Susanna's recipes for yourself so that you can experience what it might have been like to be cooking for a family in the 1870s.

At that time overtaxing of womens' brains was considered injurious to their health! Any form of higher education was out of the question. Marriage was the only desirable occupation for any woman and a well bred lady would be expected to be decorous, subservient and capable. Her husband would expect his house, even if it had been purchased with her money, to be well run and comfortable. He would expect the household accounts to balance and the children to be well cared for and a perfect advert for the family. Everything would be adjusted to his needs. To run a home well, economically and for the benefit of her husband and family, was seen to be the greatest achievement possible for a lady in Victorian days.

However, a woman of the labouring class, particularly living in industrial towns like Leek, would be expected to run a house without any help from her husband, to have children and to earn a wage . To do so well was considered to be its own reward. Small wonder that so many died young.

As now, magazines of the time were awash with useful information for women, though we suspect that if Susanna were to come across the information now so readily available in Cosmopolitan, Red or Marie Claire she would blush to the roots of her hair. 'How to run a perfect home' and 'How to instill discipline in children' were the themes most often to be found. The Leisure Hour, was a typical weekly magazine, a mix of romantic stories, articles on natural history and current events, as well as court gossip. A series of articles, written by a man of course, was entitled 'Love and Marriage' and ran for weeks and weeks. This is a taste of the advice he gave in January 1872:

> *For domestic happiness in a country clergyman's wife an ability to make a good apple dumpling and sufficient cultivation to relish Butler's Analogy may suffice. In the higher classes where there is more time to be filled up the range of accomplishments may be higher - music, a moderate taste for reading and painting......* And so it went on.

The household recipe books and account books that so many women kept give a unique insight into the day to day running of a house, the diet of the family and the food available. In any household, of course, whatever the period, tastes vary. Disposable income also influences the food that can be purchased and consumed, so the records which women kept are an important historical resource. They are an actual record of what was available and eaten, and at what cost. Although such recipe books show personal preferences and reflect regional variations some things are surprisingly constant at any given period in history, countrywide.

This book is based on the diaries, account books and recipe books, culinary and medicinal, that we found at Keele, and others that we later found in private hands. Susanna, or 'Mrs Ingleby of Basford Hall' as she would have been known in her day, lived from 1831 to 1891 through a period of very great change - perhaps experiencing greater changes in the availability and variety of food than anyone in her family before her.

During the Industrial Revolution there had been a huge shift of population from the country to the towns. In the years following it little had changed. Wages were still low and malnutrition rife - many town labourers lived close to starvation level. Potatoes, bread and dripping were the staples of their life - meat an almost unattainable luxury much of the time. The rural labourer and his family often fared little better as much of the common land that he had traditionally used had been enclosed by law.

But during Susanna's lifetime - most of the Victorian period - for the middle and upper classes, and for the 'artisan' working class with better wages, things were continually getting better. The coming of the railways from the mid 1840s revolutionised the transport of food. Fresh fish from the ports could be at inland markets in hours. In the latter half of her life the arrival of steamships, and the discovery of how to manufacture ice, made frozen meat from America and Australia a possibility, and exotic fruits became more widely available. Though she still used candles and oil lamps for lighting, and cooked on a solid fuel range, gas was now available for lighting and cooking - and electricity was soon to follow.

The technology to produce tinned and packaged food was developed in the second half of the century and, perhaps the greatest change of all, wheat became cheaper, rolled at mills, distributed nationwide - and subject to very stringent laws which prohibited its adulteration with chalk, sawdust - and things even worse. Unfortunately the milling removed the nutritious wheat germ as well, as all health conscious 20th century people came to know a hundred years later.

Susanna's recipe books reflect the landed class to which she belonged, and the county where she was born and lived all her life. When we first tried a few of the recipes - just out of curiosity really - we were surprised at how different the taste of some of the resulting dishes was. Talking to people, we found that some of the older ones remembered food very like that in Susanna's recipes. We became intrigued. Gradually the project started to snowball as more and more people became interested. Food is close to practically everyone's heart!

A few of the recipes are regional - not known outside Staffordshire. They also reflect the difference between town and country living. Susanna still bottled and preserved fruits and vegetable from her gardens, and made jam and sauces. Though available, bottled items figure hardly at all in her accounts though tinned goods do. Her London relatives lived differently, buying bottles of relishes and sauces and pots of jam. In her cookery book, as in so many of the period, the recipes for food, medicines and household hints are all jumbled up. A recipe for marmalade, for example, precedes one for a cure for a bloodshot eye on the same page. In this book we look only at Susanna's culinary recipes - the medicinal ones will have a book of their own in due course - though we do not envisage trying many of them!

VICTORIAN COOKERY

Cost of Food

Using a conversion program and picking the year 1878 randomly (prices did not vary much from year to year throughout Susanna's life) we have been able to compile a table to show the prices of many of the items she bought, in today's values. The prices of some items are very different. For example, before the advent of factory farming, eggs were expensive - the equivalent of between what would now be £1.19p to £2.17p for six. The 2002 Tesco Supermarket price is 25p for half a dozen of the cheapest eggs and only £1.25p for the top quality, large, free range ones. Chickens for the table too, for the same reason, were more expensive. Chicken was a luxury meal - quite the reverse from the everyday one it is today.

Meat and fish, on the other hand, were cheaper - best leg of lamb cost between £1.75 and £2.13 per lb - though that was still far too expensive for the average labourer. Offal, rabbits and cheese provided most of the protein in the countryside - the town labourer had meat or offal only once or twice a week if he was lucky. Herrings, however, were less than 18p each. Oysters were a cheap and nutritious meal readily available at even

Late 19th century Cheadle shops.
Nowadays meat cannot be cut up and sold on the open street.

the scruffiest pub or market stall until about 1850 when pollution and overfishing turned them into a luxury food. Today one would be hard-pushed, even with a supermarket special offer, to get lamb at under £2.75p a pound and a herring for less than 75p. Oysters are a serious luxury.

In looking at the actual price of food and other goods and comparing them with the wages which Susanna paid her servants or the men and women who did occasional work in her house and garden, one can see just how very difficult it was for a working family to afford good food. Small wonder that poaching was rife in the countryside and the health of the town dweller, for whom home-grown produce and the odd poached rabbit or pheasant was not available, was so very poor.

For those who could afford meat there were cookery books to tell the good housewife or housekeeper what to buy, how to choose it wisely, and how to cook it. Photography did not come into general use until the 1860s when people rushed to have their likenesses taken - studio portraits were fairly common by the mid 1870s. But it was a considerable time before photographs were used in books - and then they were all black and white. Hand-coloured plates were common in books by the 19th century, and colour printed plates from the middle of the century. The first commercially successful colour photos were produced in 1907, but colour photography for the masses, and in books, was to take another fifty years at least. Many of the cookery books in Susanna's time carried the same steel plate engravings. The one reproduced from Anthony Hazelmore's *The Economist or New Family Cookery*, published in 1824, is typical, and shows cuts of pork,

A plate from Anthony Hazelmore's *The Economist or New Family Cookery* published in 1824.

lamb and veal. Exactly the same engravings are found in cookery books published 40 years later in 1864, and Susanna would certainly have been familiar with this one.

Convenience foods and 'ready meals' did not exist. Pasta, such as macaroni, was plain - and the cook made her own sauce. Bulk buying, however, is not a new concept. Susanna and her sister Emily Jane, who lived nearby, tried to reduce their household expenses by doing just that. They bought tea, lard, oatmeal and apples in large quantities and split them up. An aunt in London bought an entire tea-chest of tea, dividing it between the family. Tea was expensive, the equivalent of £4.53 per pound. Herrings were bought by the box and transported directly from the fishing ports by railway and then sold on to other friends and neighbours.

Department stores sprang up in the 1860s and 1870s in response to the demand from the affluent classes and added another strand to the changing pattern of shopping habits. The Civil Service Stores were established in 1865, the Army and Navy Stores in 1871. They were co-operatives, but others, privately owned, such as Harrods and Whitelys, soon followed. For those people with sufficient money they were a boon as they sold by mail order. No longer were provincial hostesses limited by what they could buy locally. At Christmas Susanna ordered dessert raisins, macaroons and other goodies from them - had she lived now we

Department store c. 1860

A local market, and below, a fruit and vegetable cart c. 1900.

have no doubt that she would have been ordering goods over the internet - she was always willing to try new things. Susanna ordered her Christmas specialities from the Civil Service Store by post.

The variety of foods available in the 1870s and 1880s was far smaller than we now enjoy. Bananas, pineapples and other exotic fruits, although they had been imported since the 18th century, grown in the greenhouses of some stately homes, and certainly eaten at grand dinner parties, were not available to most. In Covent Garden in the 1830s pineapples could be bought, at a price, nearly all the year round, but they do not figure in any of Susanna's recipes and she does not mention having them at all - presumably they had not reached the Staffordshire market. Peaches, apricots, lemons and grapes she does mention, and we know that she grew grapes herself.

Susanna bought and used a large number of lemons - the sharpness and aromatic flavour of which had been used since medieval times in English cookery. Soft fruits and vegetables could only be bought in their season - hence the many recipes for preserving them. Cheeses were, very largely, local English ones. Towards the end of the century factory-made cheeses became available, though it is doubtful whether Susanna ever ate any of these - her cheese was bought from the local shops or farms in and around Leek.

Since chickens do not lay in the winter, and there were no heated barns or battery units, the prudent housekeeper put down eggs in buckets of lime or isinglass solution for winter use - perhaps going from farm to farm to collect enough of them. Eggs were stored in this way until well into the 20th century. Marion can remember her mother preserving eggs in a bucket which sat under the stone shelf in their pantry as a child. Susanna recorded this detail in her diary,

May 18th 1877 I put 160 eggs in lime. 5 shillings worth were from Tattons, the rest from Mr Tudor. 15 for a shilling.

May 18th 1878 I put 120 eggs in lime. 16 for a shilling bought from Mr Tudor.

Margarine had been invented by the French food technologist Mège-Mouries in 1869 but was still made almost exclusively from the caul of an ox - the softest part of oxen fat - and tasted insipid and oily. Although by 1876 many thousands of pounds of the product, euphemistically, and somewhat optimistically, known as 'butterine', were being imported from Holland, it does not seem to have made its way into any of Susanna's recipes, and for her, and her friends and family, butter, suet, lard and dripping were the fats used in their pastry, cake and pudding recipes. It was not until the 1890s that margarine was produced on any scale in this country, when a factory was started in Monstead in Cheshire. Gradually vegetable oils and groundnut oil were introduced and, by the turn of the century, it was more palatable and had found its way into working class households where, spread on bread, it became a major food source. It was a poor substitute for the vitamin rich oils from milk or meat to be found in butter or dripping, and it was to be well into the 1930s before vitamins were included which made it a useful addition to an impoverished diet.

Like everyone else at that time, Susanna grew fruit and vegetables in her garden - using and preserving all she could, giving some of the surplus to friends, neighbours and those in need and sending some to market to be sold. She listed in her diary every year her sales from the garden produce and the amount of preserves that she and her housekeeper made from fruit and vegetable marrow. Though quantities

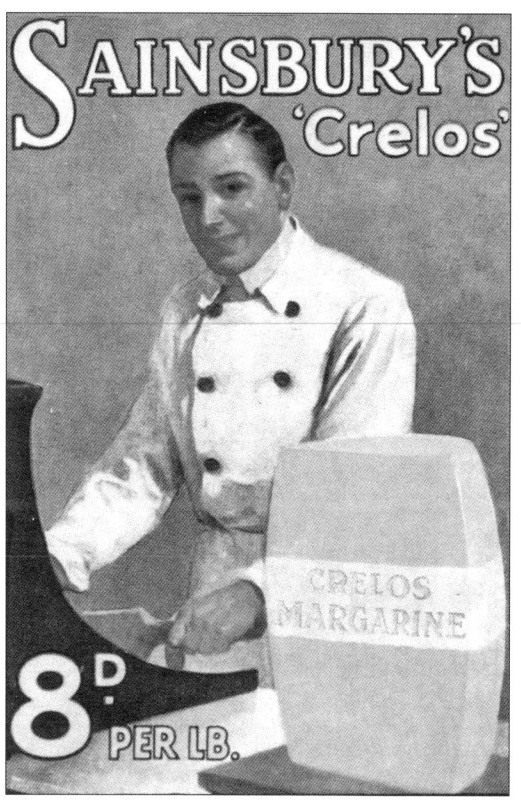

Sainsbury's margarine c 1910.

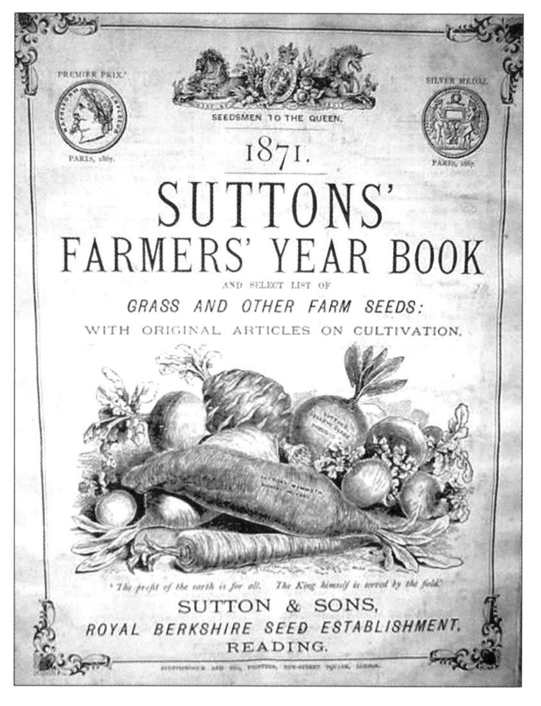

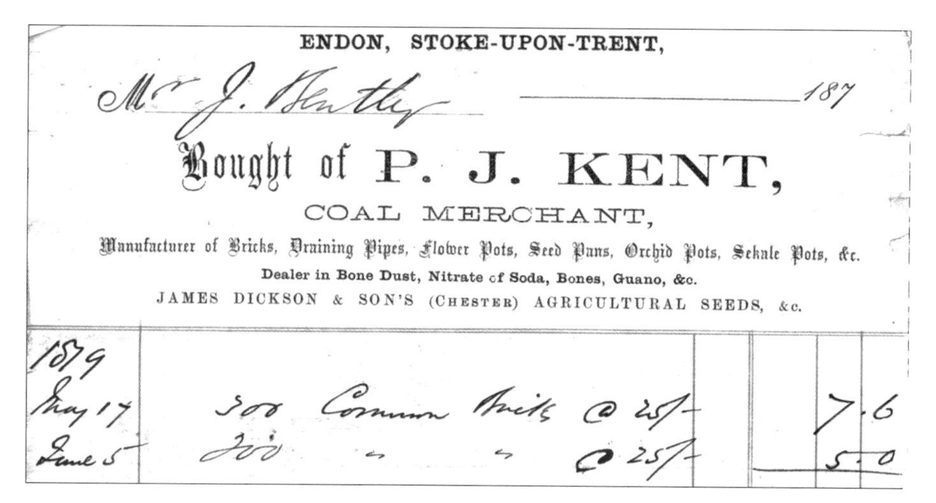
ENDON, STOKE-UPON-TRENT,

Mr J. [illegible] 187

Bought of P. J. KENT,

COAL MERCHANT,

Manufacturer of Bricks, Draining Pipes, Flower Pots, Seed Pans, Orchid Pots, Sekale Pots, &c.

Dealer in Bone Dust, Nitrate of Soda, Bones, Guano, &c.

JAMES DICKSON & SON'S (CHESTER) AGRICULTURAL SEEDS, &c.

1879		
May 17	300 Common Bricks @ 25/-	7.6
June 5	200 " " @ 25/-	5.0

varied slightly, she made the same things each year. Her accounts also show very large quantities of seeds being bought by mail order from Sutton's of Reading early in the year, and flower pots by the cart load from a Mr P. J. Kent of Endon in December. As a young child she had had a garden - her mother made sure that all her children knew how to plant seeds and reap the harvest of their labours - in poorer homes the well-tended garden patch made the real difference between an adequate diet and near starvation. But Susanna also grew luxury items:

Nov. 2nd 1878 *The last of my grapes went to Leek.*

Her odd job man Mr Harrison took the grapes to the market or fruiterers in Leek for her. She was disappointed on one occasion only to get 10d a pound for them (£1.94 in today's value) and happier another time when he got 2 shillings a pound (£4.64). She would doubtless be delighted to know that her vine still flourishes in the greenhouse at Basford Hall covering the entire roof and producing, every autumn, many pounds of luscious black grapes which her family still enjoy. We had the pleasure of tasting them one late summer evening and can vouch for their sweetness.

Game and rabbits which her brother and his friends shot during the autumn and winter shooting season also formed part of her household food. When more birds were shot than could be used they were sent to friends, whilst rabbits were often given to cottagers on the estate. Rich friends sent them gifts of venison:

Sept. 7th 1878 *John William went shooting with Colonel Philips.*
Dec. 6th 1878 *We sent a pheasant to Katie.*
Aug. 21st 1879 *Sir John Crewe sent us a haunch of venison.*

Aug 28th 1879	*Emily Jane, Miss Dora Peters and Ernest Boucher came here to eat venison with us.*
Oct. 31st 1881	*John William shot 12 rabbits with the help of Tatton's ferrets.*
Nov. 5th 1881	*We gave each of 6 cottagers a rabbit each.*
Nov. 7th 1881	*Ralph took a rabbit to Miss Alcock and read to her.*

Mrs Christine Chester of Town End Farm, Foxt, remembers serving up a very large hare when she was a little girl. She had prepared it with her mother after a cousin had shot it on the family farm. He was

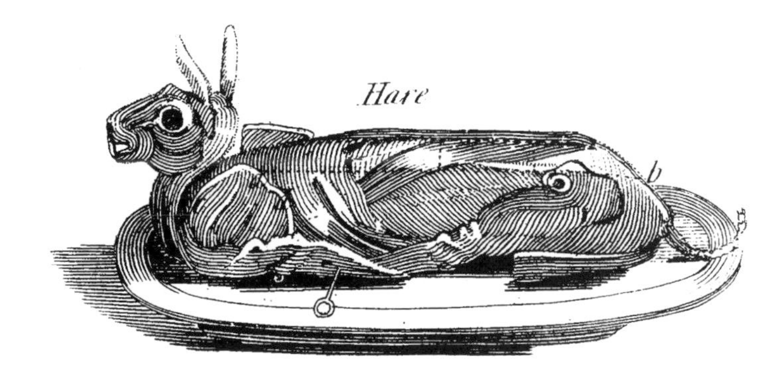

enormously proud of it, and wanted it served *'like they did in olden times'* complete with head, ears and eyes. We might nowadays be rather too squeamish to enjoy having the beast staring at us from the serving dish.

We know that Susanna also bought local meat - we have found references to *'the butcher'*, and a few items are specifically recorded - lamb, rabbits, duck and geese, but of beef there is no mention. Perhaps she ate beef that had been killed on their own farms.

Susanna was intelligent and forward looking. Her accounts reveal the very large quantity of tinned meat which she bought. Tinned beef, ox cheek, tripe, mutton and rabbit, from Australia and America, had been known for some time but by the 1870s had become readily available, as had tinned fish like sardines, salmon and lobster. She may well have opened her tins with a bull head can opener like this one.

The meat was promoted in women's magazines and the religious press as *'wholesome and inexpensive.'* It was cheaper than fresh meat and had the added advantage of being soft to chew. Perhaps that, as well as being economic, was a big part of its attraction for Susanna, as we know that she

This picture shows a French canning factory in 1860.
The men on the bench at the front of the picture are soldering the tins

frequently visited her dentist and records suffering from 'face-ache' and neuralgia'. Whatever the reason, or reasons, she bought large quantities of it - 58 pounds in 1875.

The big disadvantage, apart from its look - which we read from contemporary descriptions was greyish lumps of flesh surrounded by a watery gravy - was that the tins were soldered on the inside with lead! Although some effects of lead poisoning were recognised, Susanna, along with everyone else at the time, had no idea of the devastating effect that ingesting large quantities of tinned food with its high lead content might have - any more than in medieval times the lead glaze used on jugs and drinking vessels was known to be dangerous. Then, as in our recent past, blind faith in a food industry or government whose assurance that *'it is absolutely safe and good for you'* has led to devastating illnesses.

In 1845 two ships, Erebus and Terror, sailed for the arctic taking with them 32,018 1lb tins of meat and 17,000 tins of soup amongst other provisions. When, after 8 years, they did not return all were assumed lost. Magazines carried pictures illustrating what the ship may have looked like and speculated on what had caused the catastrophe. However, it was not until the 1970s that the bodies of the ill-fated sailors, preserved perfectly in the permafrost, were eventually found. Autopsies revealed that the entire crew of 138 officers and men in the two ships had died from lead poisoning - the result of living almost exclusively on tinned food. This engraving and the detailed information about the ships' stores and names of members of the crew, were published in *Leisure Hour Magazine* in January 1854 , though the real cause of death was not then known and it was assumed that all had perished because of cold and starvation.

From *Leisure Hour* 1854

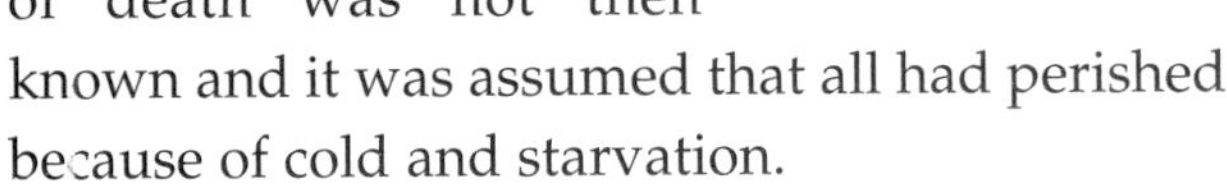

Fortunately tinned food was only a small part of the diet that Susanna and her family and servants ate, but they all suffered many undiagnosed aches and pains and feelings of general lethargy. It is just possible that this could have been partly due to mild lead poisoning from the lead in the tins of meat and fish, and in the water used for cooking and drinking which was carried in the lead water pipes put into the house in the 1830s by her father.

A can of Libby's tripe with a printed paper label c. 1880.

Then and now

Many ingredients differed from the ones we use today. The only flour available to Susanna for most of her life was plain. Self-raising flour was not produced until after 1865 and then was not widely available. Flour and oatmeal were bought by the sack from the local mill and raising or baking powder could be bought - but the thrifty housewife or cook often made her own. The flour from the mill was rather different in texture from that which we use today, coarser and with more chaff and wheat germ still in it. In consequence many of the ladies testing puddings and cakes for us have found them rather runny or sticky. Eggs were smaller. Some of our experienced cooks found they had to make adaptations to the recipes to get them to produce satisfactory results. Where this has been the case they have explained their adaptations.

Many of the puddings were boiled. Boiling produced a constant temperature that was far more easily controlled than the temperature of an oven heated by coal or wood where dampness in the wood or the quality of the coal, together with variations of wind direction and strength, made oven temperatures unpredictable and difficult to maintain. Nowadays we can set an oven temperature precisely.

The large copper pans over the fire in this picture of a typical 19th century kitchen range (which can be seen in the Victorian Museum at Newent, Gloucs) were used for for boiling puddings and stews, and are typical of the sort that Susanna would have used. The oven is but a small part of the stove.

The picture also shows an early mincing machine screwed to the table, a wooden pestle and mortar for crushing spices, and a toasting fork hanging beside the stove. Marion remembers using just such a fork when visiting her grandmother in the 1940s and is happy that she still has it. The rug in front of the fire is a rag-rug - made from scraps of old garments on a sacking base - soft, colourful and full of memories.

19th century kitchen range in the Victorian Museum at Newent

Sugar and salt were not bought by the packet or pound but by the block or loaf. Salt was grated into a pot which was usually kept beside the fire - for convenience and to keep it dry. Some of the older people we have spoken to remember grating salt being their job as children - perhaps being rewarded by being given a half penny to spend on sweets at the village store. Sugar was usually 'lump' sugar. It too came in large loaves and pieces had to be broken off with special sugar-nippers and a cleaver. It was then crushed and sifted or sieved to make it as fine as possible before being added to cakes or puddings. Without the benefit of refrigeration meat quickly became unwholesome, and recipes for dealing with this are included in many recipe books. Many people recalled how meat was sometimes soaked for a while in vinegar if it had become smelly before it was cooked. Bubble and squeak now is a vegetable dish of cabbage and potatoes: Susanna's always included meat. Potatoes also figure in a sweet pudding in Susanna's cookery book - not just as a vegetable.

Her mincemeat recipes too, as in medieval times, contained meat as well as fruit and strong spices - perhaps another way to cover the taste of any tainted meat. Susanna always made her mincemeat, in huge quantities, in November.

With few preservatives added to foods shopping was done on an almost daily basis. Larders had stone or concrete shelves where food was kept under muslin covers. Meat safes with a tent like frame covered in gauze were hung on the shady side of the house and bluebottles buzzed round in frustration. In very hot weather milk, unpasteurised and bought from the milkman by the pint jug straight from the churn on his horse-drawn cart, was kept in a bucket of water and when it did, frequently, 'go off' it was turned into curd cheese, for economy was a moral as well as a practical consideration. Nothing was wasted. Susanna would probably be horrified at our profligate attitude to food.

Bread quickly became stale and bread crumbs are to be found in many recipes, especially boiled puddings - both sweet and savoury. It was an easy and nutritious way of using them up. Many of the sweet boiled

This Food should be tried wherever other nourishment has not proved entirely satisfactory.
It is already Cooked—Requires neither boiling nor straining—Is made in a minute.

Allen & Hanburys' Infants' Food

A nutriment peculiarly adapted to the digestive organs of Infants and Young Children, supplying all that is required for the formation of firm flesh and bone. Surprisingly beneficial results have attended the use of this Food, which needs only to be tried to be permanently adopted.

"My child, after being at Death's door for weeks from exhaustion, consequent upon severe diarrhœa, and inability to retain any form of Infants' Food or Milk, began to improve immediately he took your malted preparation, and I have never seen an infant increase in weight so rapidly as he has done."—H. E. TRESTRAIL, F.R.C.S., M.R.C.P.

Further Medical Testimony and Full Directions accompanying each Tin.

Price 6d., 1s., 2s., 5s., and 10s. everywhere.

IMPORTANT CAUTION TO THE PUBLIC.—As a protection against counterfeits, see that each bears ALLEN and HANBURYS' Name.

8 Large Glasses of Delicious Custard at a Cost of 2d.

BIRD'S CUSTARD POWDER

No Luncheon, Dinner, Supper, or Feast complete without a Dish of this Favourite Custard.

In 6d. & 1s. boxes, and 2d. packets.

Recipes for Tasty Dishes enclosed in each box.

CHOICE—DELICIOUS! WITHOUT EGGS!

A GREAT LUXURY.

NO EGGS REQUIRED.

HALF THE COST—HALF THE TROUBLE.

"PASTRY AND SWEETS" POST FREE.

ALFRED BIRD and SONS, BIRMINGHAM, will send, on receipt of address, the new and enlarged edition of "PASTRY AND SWEETS," a little work containing practical hints and original recipes for tasty dishes for dinner and supper

FOUR GOLD MEDALS AWARDED.

Goddard's Plate Powder

NON-MERCURIAL.

THE BEST AND SAFEST article for CLEANING SILVER and ELECTRO-PLATE. Sold in Boxes, 1s., 2s. 6d., and 4s. 6d. each, by Grocers and Oilmen everywhere.

HOME, SWEET HOME!

The Sweetest Homes are those where HUDSON'S EXTRACT OF SOAP is in daily use.
HUDSON'S EXTRACT OF SOAP for all Waters, Hard, Cold, Soft, or Hot. HUDSON'S SOAP saves Time, Labour, Money, Wear, and Tear.

REMARKABLE DISAPPEARANCE! of all dirt from everything by using HUDSON'S EXTRACT of SOAP. See that you get HUDSON'S, the only genuine. In fine powder. For all domestic Washing, Cleansing, and Scouring. Lathers freely. Softens Water. Leaves no smell. Packets ONE PENNY everywhere.

Tonga

The SPECIFIC for NEURALGIA.

"Tonga maintains its reputation in the treatment of Neuralgia."—*Lancet*.

"Invaluable in facial Neuralgia. Has proved effective in all those cases in which we have prescribed it."—*Medical Press*.

2s. 9d., 4s. 6d., and 11s. Of all Chemists.

By Special Royal and Imperial Warrant.

EGERTON BURNETT'S ROYAL SERGES

PATTERNS FREE. PARCELS CARRIAGE PAID.

NEW PATTERN BOOKS POST FREE.

ANY LENGTH SOLD.

FOR LADIES', CHILDREN'S, AND GENTLEMEN'S DRESS. UNSURPASSED FOR BEAUTY, NOVELTY, AND STERLING VALUE. UNAFFECTED BY EITHER THE SUN OR SALT WATER.

JUBILEE SERGE. A new make woven from the finest Colonial Wools of exceptionally long fibre, of far greater strength than ordinary soft fabrics. The best ever offered for wear and soft texture. In the fashionable shades at 1s. 11½d. yard.

EGERTON BURNETT'S Royal Serge Warehouse
WELLINGTON, SOMERSET, ENGLAND.

A few Reasons why

CADBURY'S COCOA *(Registered)*

Enjoys such World-Wide Popularity.

It is guaranteed to be pure Cocoa.
It is soluble in boiling milk or water.
It contains all the delicious aroma of the natural article, without the excessive proportions of fat.
It is not reduced in value by the addition of Starch, Sugar, Etc.
It is specially rich in flesh-forming and strength-sustaining principles.
It is a gentle stimulant, and sustains against hunger and bodily fatigue.
It is delicious, nutritious, digestible, comforting, and a refined beverage suitable for all seasons of the year.
In the whole process of manufacturing Cadbury's Pure Cocoa, the automatic machinery employed obviates the necessity for its being once touched by the human hand.

PURE

PRECAUTION AND WARNING.

Always ask for Cadbury's Cocoa. Always examine your purchase. See that you have not been induced to accept an imitation, as the great esteem in which Cadbury's Cocoa is held has led to the most unscrupulous Copying of Labels and Packages, for the sake of extra profit.

Be wary of highly-coloured and drugged preparations offered as pure Cocoa. Anything of a medicated character associated with Cocoa proclaims it at once to be an imposture.

PARIS DEPOT—90, RUE ST. HONORE.

What shall I Drink?

The *Lancet* says:—"We counsel the public to drink their Lime Juice whenever and wherever they list. As a rule, Lime Juice is, particularly during the summer, a far more wholesome drink than any form of alcohol. We have subjected the samples of the 'Lime Fruit Juice' of the Montserrat Company to full analysis, with a view to test its quality and purity. WE HAVE FOUND IT TO BE IN SOUND CONDITION AND ENTIRELY FREE FROM ADULTERATION."

MONTSERRAT

LIME-FRUIT JUICE AND CORDIALS.

Limetta, or Pure Lime Juice Cordial

Aromatic, Clove, Strawberry, Raspberry, Pineapple, Sarsaparilla, Jargonelle, Peppermint.

In vogue at all Christmas and New Year's Parties, Balls, Assemblies, &c.

CAUTION.—The success of the above has caused many IMITATIONS to spring up, many of them UTTERLY WORTHLESS Concoctions. It is therefore of the utmost importance to traders as well as the Public to see that the trade marks of the MONTSERRAT COMPANY (Limited), and the SOLE CONSIGNEES, are on the Capsule of each Bottle. The word "Montserrat," is also duly registered as a trade mark. Legal proceedings will be instituted against all persons infringing the Trade Marks as above named.—Sole Consignees, EVANS, SONS and CO., Liverpool.

THE LATEST NOVELTY FOR HOUSE DECORATION!

The "Lancaster" Window-Blind Cloth.

ELEGANCE! DURABILITY! UTILITY! ECONOMY!

PLAIN COLOURS. FANCY PATTERNS. ARTISTIC DESIGNS.

Charming Combinations of Shades to match Modern Furniture and Decorations. Requires no Washing. Will Sponge Clean, Does not Crease, May be Cut to any Width without Fraying, Rolls up Straight. No Hemming, Not liable to Fade, Will stand Rough Wear, Is unaffected by Heat, Damp, or Exposure to the Weather.

Two New Patterns for 1887 are specially in honour of THE QUEEN'S JUBILEE and give handsome views of the Royal Palaces, Portraits of the Royal Family, &c.

They are Novel, Beautiful, and Durable. Can be had in all Widths, 28 to 72 in.

☞ PROCURABLE FROM ALL DRAPERS, UPHOLSTERERS, AND CABINET MAKERS.

An advertising page from *The Graphic* Magazine of 1887

puddings that we have tried which are made this way are light and delicious. Scraps of fat were rendered down, old pieces of dried-out cheese were grated and used up in, or on, supper dishes.

'Waste is a serious evil when so large a proportion of the community often procure, even with painful difficulty and sustained labour, insufficient bread to sustain existence...' wrote Eliza Acton in 1864. She was the Delia Smith of her day and everyone had her books. She went on, at some considerable length, to extol the virtue of *'wholesome and well cooked food'* above *'fancy and fashionable food served only to impress'*, though some of the recipes in her books belie this. *'Eat to live'* was her motto. A huge row broke out between Eliza Acton and the other great cookery writer of the time Isabella Beeton - known to everyone as Mrs Beeton. In 1855 Eliza had written a furious preface to an updated version of her book, *'I have amended 'Author's Recipe' to 'Authors Original Recipe' in defence of the unscrupulous manner in which large portions of my volumes have been appropriated by contemporary authors* (she meant Mrs Beeton) *without the slightest acknowledgement......at present I am suffering too great a penalty for the over-exertion entailed on me to see strangers coolly taking the credit and the profits....'*

Poor Eliza was obviously somewhat justified as a comparison of the texts of both authors makes clear. Mrs Beeton certainly was extremely familiar with Eliza Acton's recipes - and also benefited from having a publisher for a husband!

Weights and measures

Weight was measured in stones, pounds and ounces:

16 ounces = 1 pound   14 pounds = 1 stone

Volume was measured in quarts, pecks and bushels, for dry food and liquid:

2 pints = 1 quart   4 quarts = 1 gallon
4 gallons = 1 peck   4 pecks = 1 bushel

We hardly ever use pecks and bushels now - but gallons are still widely understood and we still have pint cartons of milk. The milk advertising slogan of 1958 'Drinka pinta milka day' is widely remembered.

Susanna regularly bought blackberries, red currants and bilberries by the quart, though she also purchased redcurrants by the pound. In

Finland today soft fruits in the markets are measured in litres (a little less than a quart). A quart of blackberries, we discovered, weighs about one pound. It seems to be an easy and practical way to measure such squashy fruit. Apples were often bought by the peck. This measurement varied a little from place to place but a peck was about 2 gallons. Picking apples straight into a 2 gallon bucket in the orchard and then tipping them into a sack would seem to be a practical way to pick, transport and sell apples without the unnecessary complication of scales. And, as today, some things were sold individually - lemons, oranges and herrings for example.

The Recipes

The recipes are quoted exactly as they are written in Susanna's recipe book. Cooking temperatures are vague and we suggest you consult your own cookery books to convert the gas and electricity ones given by our testers.

We have not attempted to include all Susanna's recipes. Some are now obsolete - the ingredients unobtainable or difficult to come by - for example pigs-fry (a pig's heart, liver, intestines and testicles), medlars, and New Zealand tinned mutton. Some would possibly now be unpalatable - savoury tripe, hung beef, cow-heel jelly - though one man we spoke to remembers his father taking a mug of set cow-heel jelly and a spoon down the mine each day. Some are simply not relevant any more now that we are able to obtain eggs, vegetables and fruit all year round. Who now would want to spend time making baking powder or preserving lettuce stalks or green peas? We do not need to be told that 'salt brings out flavour' - a new idea in Susanna's time - indeed our food is now perhaps overloaded with salt, and we certainly do not need the recipe to see if our milk has been watered down. Food adulteration was a serious hazard in Susanna's day and no doubt there were unscrupulous tradesmen who diluted their milk. She carefully recorded:

The following plan for testing milk for adulteration is recommended for its simplicity. Dip a well polished knitting needle into a deep vessel of milk and immediately withdraw it in an upright position. If the milk is pure some of the fluid will adhere to the needle: should water have been added there will be no adhesion of fluid.

Stafford Record Office abounds with accounts of prosecutions brought against dishonest traders in the 1870s and 1880s. Marion put her supermarket skimmed milk to the test and was relieved to find that it passed - the milk adhered to the knitting needle!

Now it is time for you to meet Susanna. This photograph was

taken in London in 1872 by Elliott and Fry - well-known society photographers. Susanna was on a visit to the capital - mainly to support her brother John William who was undergoing expensive, lengthy and painful experimental treatment for his *'quinsy throat'*.

Mrs Susanna Ingleby

We have arranged this book so that you will learn something of her story as we follow her to the various places in Staffordshire where she lived: Basford, Cheddleton, Oakamoor, Armitage and Abbots Bromley, and other towns and villages associated with her like Foxt, Cheadle, Leek and Rugely.

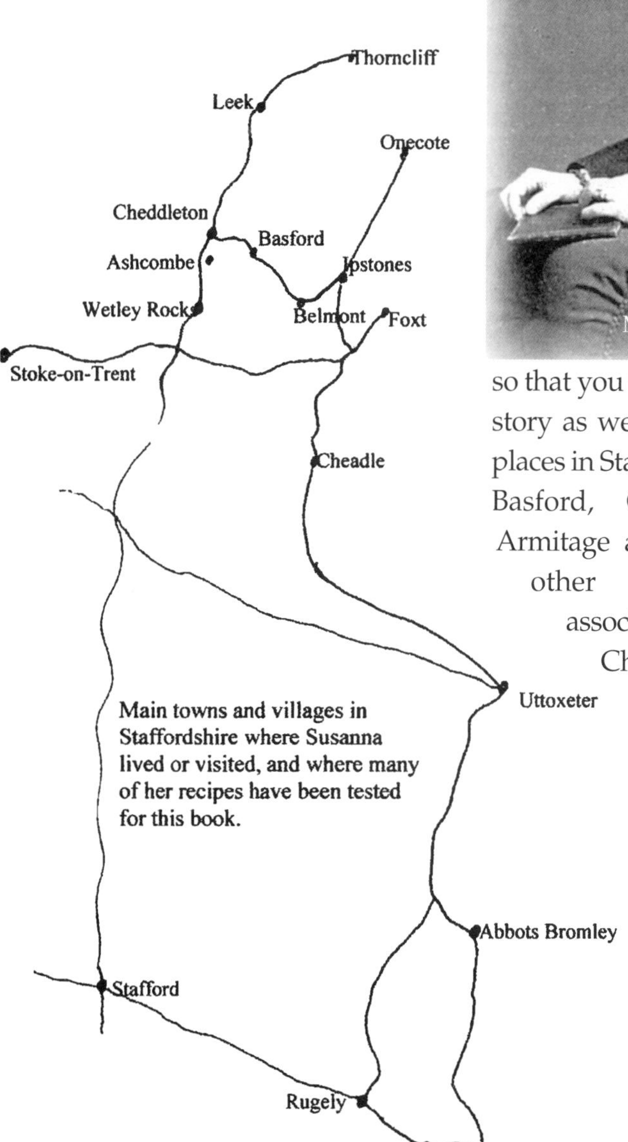

Main towns and villages in Staffordshire where Susanna lived or visited, and where many of her recipes have been tested for this book.

During the journey you will meet members of her family and many other Staffordshire people who have tried her recipes for us and told us their memories of food. Our book is a human as well as a culinary journey. We hope you enjoy it.

A list of all Susanna's Culinary and Household Recipes

(We have not included her medicinal recipes)

Vegetable recipes

Boiled carrots and turnips
Browning onions etc.
Croquettes of potatoes
Fried vegetable marrow
Frying onions
Haricot beans
Haricot fritters
Peas pudding
Potato cakes
Rice and peas
Scalloped tomatoes
To boil Rice (Patna)
To keep vegetables a good colour

Preserves and sauces

Apple sauce
A gravy
Browning
Cow heel jelly
Damson cheese
Eggs in lime
Gooseberry jelly
Marmalade
Kidney beans in winter
Medlar jelly
Mince meat
Mint Sauce
Parsley butter
Mrs Freer's walnut catsup
Raspberry acid
Raspberry vinegar
Salad dressing
To Preserve eggs (in salt)
To preserve eggs for winter use
To preserve Green peas all the year
To preserve lettuce stalks
To preserve French beans green 2 recipes
Vegetable marrow preserve
Lemon cheese to keep 12 months

Soups

Abbots Bromley soup
A nice addition to clear soup
Clear vegetable soup
Lentil soup
Milk soup
Mulligatawny soup
Mutton broth
Old green pea soup
Pea soup old
Vegetable marrow soup

Meat dishes

Character of good meat
To make tough meat tender (2 recipes)
To make fresh meat tender
For freshening tainted meat
To rend down scraps of fat
Australian meat - defence of
Bubble and squeak
Grilled Bull's kidneys
Grilled steaks
Haricot mutton
Hung beef
Irish stew
New Zealand meat
Beef stew
Poor man's goose
Rissoles
Sausage rolls
Sea pie
Sheep's heart
Toad in the hole
To stew a loin of mutton
Tripe

Vegetarian Recipes

Cauliflower and cheese
Cheese and rice
Cheese faggots
Cheese fritters
Cheese macaroni
Corn oysters
Lentil cutlets
Macaroni and cheese
Substitute for suet
Savoury trifle
Scalloped eggs
To make cream cheese
Tomatoes and cheese
To stew macaroni
Vegetable pie

Puddings and cakes etc.

Ale jelly
Almond pudding
Apple dumplings
Apple paste
Apple turnovers
Baking powder
Arrowroot blancmange
Banbury buns
Batter for fritters
Belmont cakes
Biscuits
Bath buns
Batter for fritters
Buttermilk
Pikelets very good
Canary pudding
Corn flour on bread & preserves
Garden of Eden pudding
Egg pudding
Gingerbread cakes
Gateau des Pommes delicious
Ginger bread
Oatcakes
Live loring (a rhubarb dish)
Macaroni pudding
Orange Delight
North Staffordshire Fermity
Oz pudding
Plum pudding
Plain baked plum pudding
Potato pudding
Rhubarb
Rice mould
Rowsley pudding
Scones
Shrewsbury cakes
Sponge cakes
Stewed pears
Swiss cream
Tapioca cream (cold)
To Make Rattifee cakes
Transparent pudding
Treacle pudding
White blancmange
Wholemeal cakes

Drinks

Apple water
Barley cream
Barley water
Beef tea
Bran tea
Cocoa
Ginger pop
Lime water
Quick beef tea
Something to drink (2 recipes)

Miscellaneous culinary recipes

Salt brings out flavour
Snow and eggs
Testing for Milk adulteration. Medical Examiners' Stafford Papers 1878

Miscellaneous household recipes

Against mould
For cleaning Britannia metal goods
For cleaning fire-irons
For polishing wood and leather
For renovating black dresses
For rusty grates
For varnishing furniture
Steel ointment to remove rust
To clean a boiler
To get rid of rats
To mend china
To prevent clothes fading in washing
To prevent a wick from smoking
To brighten steel
To ornament a table
To remove ink stains

One
BASFORD

Basford Hall

Susanna

Susanna was born at Basford Hall near Cheddleton in 1831. She was the seventh child and the fifth daughter to be born to the Reverend John Sneyd and his wife Penelope. This picture is a painting made of the hall at about that time. Eventually she would be one of 14 children. Hers was an unremarkable childhood, typical of that of many children brought up in a wealthy landed family. The Sneyds owned a large estate, had twelve live-in servants and a carriage with the family coat of arms on it when Susanna was young. Her father was an important man, for as well as being the vicar of Ipstones he was also a magistrate and the first Rural Dean of Leek.

Though the adults would have had large joints of meat, cheeses, tarts and puddings, the children had very different food and ate in the nursery upstairs. Milky puddings, bread and butter and boiled puddings would have been deemed suitable nursery food. And it was none too plentiful. Susanna's eldest sister Penelope recalled that there was never enough for second helpings and her brother John William complained in later life that his digestion had been ruined as even as a young adult he was allowed to eat meat only on alternate days throughout the year. The practice was insisted on by their domineering father who seemed to have considered it their Christian duty, even though it was not standard Anglican practice. No meat on Fridays was a Roman Catholic and High Anglican custom to commemorate Good Friday - but the Reverend John seems to have gone beyond that.

Basford Hall, just outside Cheddleton and near Leek, overlooks wonderful scenery in the valley of the River Churnet. Susanna later wrote that there was nowhere on earth as beautiful as the Staffordshire countryside. Basford Hall is still owned by members of the Sneyd family, Humphrey and Judy Scott-Moncrieff. Many family portraits that Susanna would recognise still hang there. The ice house, a wonderful egg-shaped construction, built into the side of the steep hill, is still there and in perfect order. A local bricklayer, Mr Goldstraw, constructed it for Susanna's father in 1830, and in her childhood ice would have been stored there, collected from frozen rivers and ponds in the winter, carted up by the barrow load, to be tipped into the icehouse and used to make iced puddings in the summer or keep meat fresh that had been killed on the farm.

Judy Scott-Moncrieff

Whilst she was a child Susanna was expected, along with her brothers and sisters, to make the gruelling trek up to Ipstones - about 3 miles uphill - each Sunday to hear her father preach. She was a devout Anglican and the church became her mainstay and a great comfort throughout her life. Quite a lot of her childhood was not spent at home but with with her Aunt Mary, her father's only sister, at Highfields near Uttoxeter, where she shared lessons with her cousins. She also went away to school in London for a short time.

Education was important in her family for the girls as well as boys - which was not the case in all wealthy families. Girls were expected to be able to sew and cook and read. Writing, for village girls, was not considered important. For well-bred young ladies reading, writing, painting, singing, a knowledge of French and some English history formed the curriculum. It was not deemed attractive to be too intelligent or knowledgeable. The men had to be able to shine.

Aged 13, in the summer of 1844, she spent the summer in Wales with her family at the tiny village of Beddgelert, near Snowdon, where her father had leased a copper mine in partnership with his father and eldest son, John William. It must have been an exciting time and a relief after the great sadness in February of that year when her 16 year old sister Helen, the nearest girl to her in age, died of consumption.

It was a glorious summer. All the family, with cart-loads of belongings, cooking utensils and family servants made the three day trip to the house her father had rented, and, once there, Susanna joined her brothers and sisters in rowing on the lakes and picnicking in the meadows. She visited historic sites, went to the local church, and, one memorable night, climbed to the top of Snowdon and spent the night there - waiting for sunrise with her father, brother John William and older sisters Penelope, Harriet and Emily Jane. When morning came they made their way down, the girls wearing the tight boots, voluminous undergarments and long full skirts of respectable Victorian ladies.

But the mine was a disaster. Having taken no advice until it was too late, and aggravating the local miners beyond endurance with his arrogance, her father lost all his money in a bitter court case - heard in Welsh and conducted against him and his partners by Welsh lawyers - the miners were awarded over a million pounds in today's money!

This difficult time was made worse by the death, in 1849, of Susanna's mother Penelope. She was almost 50. With many children still at home Susanna's father quickly remarried - but his new wife, Mary, was little older than Susanna. Relationships at home were difficult. On the death of Susanna's grandfather, in 1851, her father inherited Ashcombe Park and she moved there with him and his new wife. Shortly afterwards Ada Mary, her half-sister, was born.

They lived there for only a short time. Facing financial ruin, her father tried to mortgage the entire family estate to raise money. John William, his son, who had seen at first hand the debacle in Wales, opposed him. A bitter argument erupted - the Reverend John was not used to being thwarted - but John William had been left part of the estate by his grandfather and the Reverend John needed his son's agreement. John William refused. Furious, his father banished him from the family home in the middle of the night into the pouring rain. Their bitter quarrel was never resolved, John William was disinherited, and the terrible family problems that ensued dogged Susanna for the rest of her life.

Recipes

The twins, Alexandra and William Scott-Moncrieff, are Susanna's great-great-great-great nephew and niece, and live in her old home Basford Hall. They made the ginger pop from Susanna's cookery book with help from their mother, Judy Scott-Moncrieff, using old fashioned scales and weights, and tried it out on some of their friends.

Though bottled ginger beer was available in Susanna's time it is almost certain that at Basford it would have been freshly made to serve at the croquet and archery and picnic parties held there in the summer. This recipe was given to Susanna by her stepmother, Mary Sneyd, on July 22nd 1866. Susanna was on holiday at Basford. She wrote in her diary, *'Fine and hot. Mrs Walter Smith came in the afternoon for croquet. Mary, Emily, Henry and I shot* [arrows]. *We all had tea in the Fox Plantation.'*

Alexandra and William Scott-Moncrieff

Basford Hall Ginger Pop **Mary Sneyd**

I lb loaf sugar broken small but not powdered.
1 oz cream of tartar.
The rinds of 2 lemons. 1 oz of whole or ground ginger.
Pour on this 1 gallon of boiling water.
Stir well and when nearly cold add the juice of the 2 lemons and 1 tablespoon of fresh yeast.
Stir well and let all settle. Strain throe' a cloth into stone bottles.
Tie down the corks.
It will be ready to drink in 12 hours.

Mary Sneyd, Susanna's Stepmother

Judy - the pop was easy to make though I'd probably add a little a little more sugar if we make it again. We used wine bottles for storage. It does not keep particularly well getting sharper the longer it is kept.

Alexandra - 'I thought that the ginger beer was very nice but it was not very fizzy and it was also rather sour, but I still liked it. It was yummy.'

William - 'Delicious, but it didn't look appetising. After a while it started to make your tongue and throat go hot. It was the best ginger beer I've ever tasted.'

Alice and George Mitchell (5 year old twin school friends of William and Alexandra): 'We liked it. It wasn't too sweet and is the best ginger beer we've had.'

Alice and George Mitchell

Food Memories in Basford

Just down the hill from Basford Hall is Basford Hurst. It was once a grand private house, where Susanna used to exhibit flowers and vegetables she had grown at Basford, in the annual garden show held there.

It is now a spacious nursing home where Averil Scott-Moncrieff, grandmother of the Scott-Moncrieff twins, is a contented resident. We asked several of the other residents what they could remember of food in their childhood.

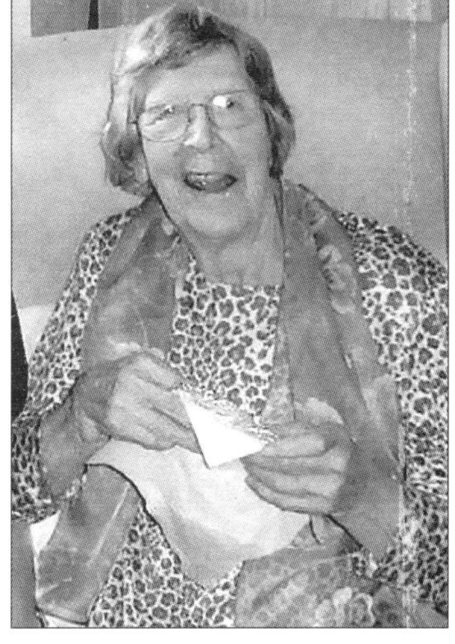

Averil Scott-Moncrieff

Connie Heath, aged 91, born near Ashbourne, Derbyshire

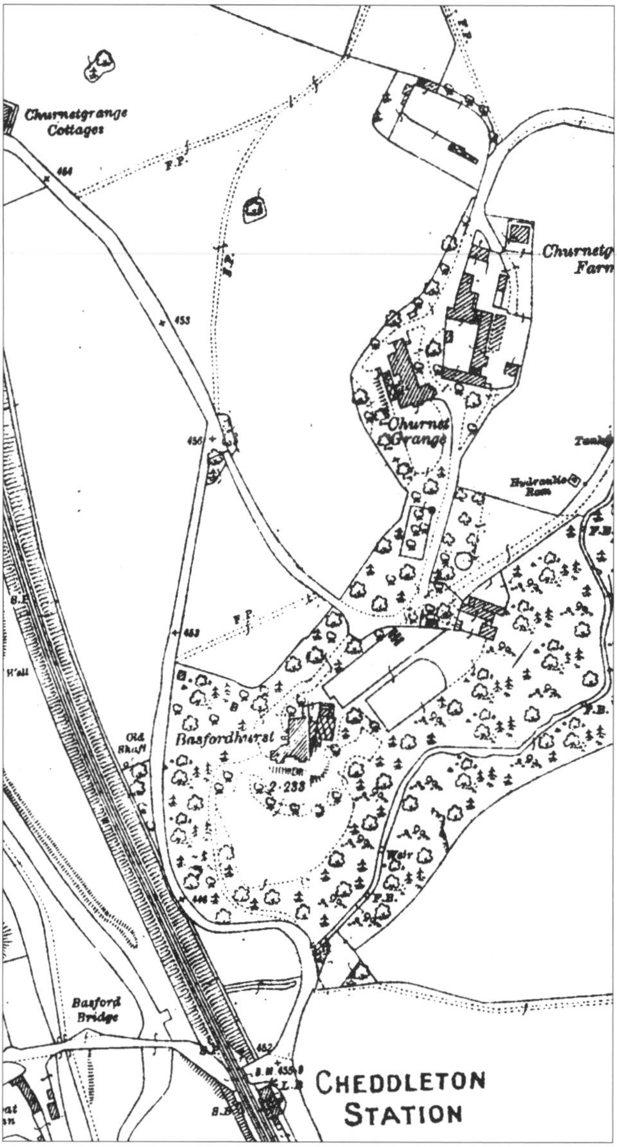

"I was one of 9 children. My parents had a small farm but father died when I was 10 and mother carried on alone. My job was to look after the poultry - we raised turkeys for the Christmas market and had one ourselves. They were smaller and thinner than the ones today but they did get bigger when we understood more about feeding them. We only had one thin slice of breast for our Christmas dinner - it was a real treat. In our Christmas stocking we had an orange an apple and some chocolate and a toy or game.

Each market day the trap went to Ashbourne and left orders at the grocers for flour, oatmeal, sugar and sometimes dried fruit. Our mother made all our bread and cakes, especially lardy cake, a rich cake made with currants and dripping. I mainly remember bread and milk for breakfast and supper, made with stale bread, hot milk and salt. Sometimes we had porridge or oatcakes instead. We took sandwiches for our lunch at school - usually dripping and sometimes with a bit of bacon.

Our main meal was on Saturday when we had a joint from the local butcher. We dipped bread in the lovely gravy, then our mother left the meat to go cold and we had it sliced. It went further that way as it had to last for the rest of the week with potatoes, bread and cabbage. You'd call it bubble and squeak now -

I don't know why. Mother made her own butter and a sort of cream cheese which sometimes went mouldy - but there was still never any left over! We had apple and damson trees in the garden and mother made damson jam.

Dad grew vegetables, mainly cabbage and potatoes, and after he died we all helped in the garden. When I grew up I became a teacher."

Another resident, Marjorie Alice Carr aged 92

Marjorie had a very different childhood from Connie being one of 2 children and brought up in Leek. Her story engrossed us and brings close a style of life which seems so far distant to us.

Marjorie was born in Leek in 1919 and had one sister. She lived in the area all her life retiring to Cheddleton with her mother, and then living alone for the last 14 years after her mother died. A bright child, she won a scholarship to Westwood Girls' School, in Leek, but her whole life seemed to be blighted by a careless remark made by her geography teacher one day. *"In front of the whole class, she said, 'Marjorie Carr you are a very stupid girl.' And I believed her. I believed her."*

Marjorie had wanted to be a teacher but she ended up as a clerk in Leek where she was the only person in the office. It was a very lonely job. Travellers called but she was by herself most of the time and meeting very few people. To this day she regards herself, sadly, as stupid - which quite plainly she is not.

Her most vivid childhood memory is one of being constantly short of money. To make ends meet her mother worked at home for the local silk mill, finishing silk scarves by putting the fringing on them. Her wages were pitifully small. It was Marjorie's job to go to the mill after school and fetch the scarves for her mother and sometimes she deliberately did not bring any back, telling her mother that there were none that day as she could not bear to see her working so hard for so little money. Their one big treat each year was a day trip to Blackpool.

A silk mill in Leek

Food was plain and with no refrigeration shopping was done daily from the local shops. Breakfast was usually porridge. Suppers were sometimes fish, sometimes cheese on toast, or brains on toast with salt and pepper, or often just dripping and salt and pepper on toast hot from the fire. Marjorie told us how it was her job to clean the brains, a job which she found quite satisfying. *"You washed them in salted water, untangled them and pulled off all the loose bits of pink skin."* Pigs trotters and sweetbreads were other family dishes.

Most of the nursing home's care attendants, who were listening with interest to Marjorie's memories, had never had sweetbreads and asked what they were. There was some confusion and embarrassment as one of the older assistants said to Marjorie, very loudly, for she is hard of hearing, *"They were lamb's testicles weren't they Marjorie?"*

"What?"

"Testicles", she repeated, adding graphic pictures with her fingers to the obvious puzzlement of the residents who had not heard the beginning of the conversation - *"You know, the dangly bits!"*

The room dissolved into laughter. Pigs' trotters, brains and sweetbreads were common and staple food in the 1930s but are not frequently eaten now in this country - in fact brains are not available because of BSE. Pigs' trotters are still available - they are stripped off and used in pies after boiling, though a butcher told us he had difficulty in giving them away now.

He still sells some sweetbreads which he described as *"an acquired taste"*. Pam's reply was, *"Rubbish, I LOVE them!"* They have to be blanched in milk and are then usually fried after being coated in breadcrumbs. Brains, sweetbreads and trotters were often regarded as 'poor men's food'. In this country now - but not across the Channel - they are thought of as foods that belong to another age. Susanna would have known them well.

In the summer when there was a glut of runner beans, Marjorie told us -remembering it with relish - there would often be just fresh beans and bread and butter for supper. Her mother baked all their cakes using lard or margarine, though she bought oatcakes and pikelets, and sometimes a ginger bun as a special treat. They even tried to make their own chocolate using cocoa solids and cocoa butter. Main meals were simple, stewed rabbit, rabbit pie and 'lobby'.

"What's lobby, Marjorie?" we asked.

"You don't know what lobby is? Well it's, well, lobby. You know, a sort of meat stew with vegetables and barley."

For pudding there was often a roly-poly pudding with syrup or a little dried fruit. The family diet was greatly enriched by the produce her father grew in his greenhouse, including mushrooms, and she does not remember ever having been hungry.

It appears lobby is still a familiar word in North Staffordshire and was a dish that traditionally was kept on the go all day, or sometimes longer, and could contain any vegetable or meat that was 'left over' - a real 'stew'. We had not come across the name before, but it is obviously a well known local name as it was recognised by even the young nursing staff in the home. One recalled her grandmother making it - *"a rich thick stew - lovely on a cold winter evening after school - always on the hob."* We were to come across it again later the same day.

How easily food takes us far back into history. In her book *Food in Britain* (1954, Macmillan) Dorothy Hartley describes and gives the recipe for a dish called Lobcouse, indicating that lob = sheep and couse = broth:

Lobcouse

Dust the neck of lamb in flour and brown it in the bottom of a heavy pan. Put on top root vegetables, carrots, turnip and a few parsnips and swedes cut up. Sprinkle with mountain herbs and barley. Add sliced potatoes and then whole potatoes. Fill with water up to the whole potatoes but do not cover them. Put the lid on the pot and simmer gently until all is cooked. Do not open the lid or stir. The sliced potatoes will be reduced to a creamy mass so thickening the broth. Serve straight from the pot. (The longer the cooking the better.)

The Oxford English Dictionary has the word 'lobcouse' meaning a sailor's stew: meat and vegetables topped with ship's biscuits - perhaps the origin of Susanna's Sea Pie (see p. 90), the only difference being that hers was topped with a suet crust. It goes on to say that in Dutch the word is lapkous, and in Danish, German and Norwegian lapskaus. It does not specify the meat as lamb.

The soup served by Susanna and the other gentry ladies at Abbots Bromley, which you can read about in the Abbots Bromley chapter, was almost certainly a variation of lobby, and last summer, in the far north of

Norway, Marion was able to sample a Viking dish in the reconstruction of a Viking chieftain's house. From a huge iron pot suspended over an open fire, with the smoke curling up to the high rafters above, she had a delicious meat stew with vegetables, barley, and wild thyme. And it was served with oatcakes!

When we went to Leek and talked to elderly residents there they talked with relish of lobby and oatcakes. To this day oatcakes are a North Staffordshire speciality and there is still an oatcake shop which makes them freshly every day and another which sells lobby in foil dishes to take home and reheat. Perhaps lobby and oatcakes were Viking dishes brought over when they settled here, in the North of England. Only some were the 'pillagers' so depicted by history - many were honest farmers looking for new land to farm. The recipe has been handed down through the ages - probably the lobcouse or lapkaus being gradually corrupted to 'lobby'.

Leek people queue outside this little shop on a Sunday morning for fresh oatcakes

Sharpcliffe Hall in the recent past.

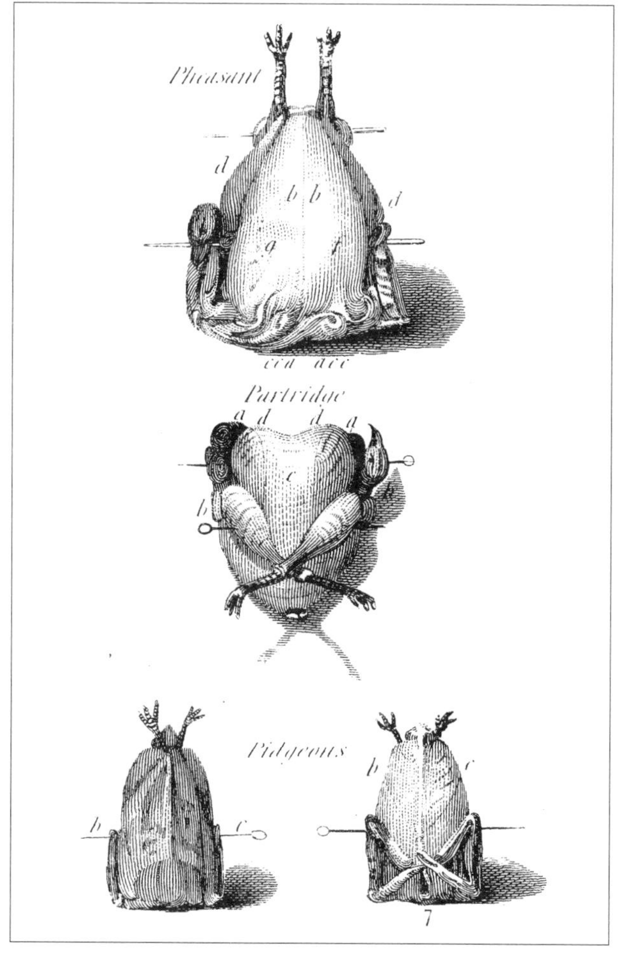

Two
CHEDDLETON and WETLEY ROCKS

Susanna

During her teens and early twenties Susanna lived in several of the houses on the Sneyd estate. One was Sharpcliffe - a beautiful 17th century farmhouse with extensive land which her father bought for her brother Ralph to farm in 1845 - largely with money borrowed from his sister Mary. And it was whilst she and Emily Jane were staying with their brothers at Sharpcliffe in 1859 that Susanna was first seen by her future husband, the Reverend Charles Ingleby. But Susanna lived mainly at Woodlands, a substantial house in the grounds of Ashcombe Park which was built in 1832 for her father's brother Tom, and from which she was married in 1860. She also lived briefly at Ashcombe Park itself - the impressive Georgian style mansion built by her grandfather in 1808.

Whilst at Woodlands Susanna and her sister Emily Jane taught sewing in the villages of Cheddleton and nearby Wetley Rocks at local schools. They often attended Cheddleton Church and were close friends with the vicar and his wife. Nestling in the valley of the River Churnet, Cheddleton was a very different village from the one we see today. It was smaller, only 370 people, but there was plenty of industry with busy paper and flint mills, and the canal which runs through Cheddleton was alive

Woodlands

with barges carrying ore, coal and other goods.

Although only about 3 miles from Leek the village had many shops: 3 butchers, 4 shoe shops, 6 other general shops and a tailor. Many of the shops sold beer as well as provisions. The Red Lion, in which John Sneyd held a magistrate's court, still serves food and drink to the village, and the Black Lion still sits facing the village church.

The station which Susanna and her family frequently used was opened in 1845, reputedly designed by Pugin. It is still there and now the centre of a preserved steam railway.

The Caldon Canal at Cheddleton.

Recipes

Some of the ladies from Cheddleton WI - Hilda Kirkham and Doreen Hughes are pictured - tried out three vegetarian dishes for us. Susanna had many vegetarian recipes in her book as her nephew Ralph decided to become a vegetarian as a young adult. (see Ralphy Connection chapter)

Milk Soup

3 pints of water.
4 leeks boiled until quite tender and 4 potatoes.
When quite soft rub them through a sieve. 3 oz butter.
Put this back into the saucepan with half a pint of milk.

Cheddleton Station

The bridge over the canal at Cheddleton.

Wetley Rocks

When it boils sprinkle in 2 oz fine sago. Boil 10 minutes.

Comment: Somewhat bland, but quite pleasant. We had warm crusty baps with ours. Perhaps more herbs would have helped.

Hilda Kirkham & Doreen Hughes

Corn Oysters *Miss Studdy*

Boil some haricot beans until tender.
Chop them not too small.
Mix a small quantity of lentils, boiled, half a cup of bread crumbs.
Ditto of fine flour, parsley and onion.
Mix all together with 2 eggs as you would a batter.
Fry them in oil keeping them the shape of an oyster as much as possible.
Add pepper to taste and serve with lemon.

Comment: 'We didn't like them.'

Eds. 'The method is vague - presumably they are called Corn Oysters for the shape. Mrs Beeton has a similar recipe, equally vague as regards quantities, *'Boiled haricot beans, any that are leftover from the day before will do'*, she says, rather unenthusiastically. Marion tried them.'

4 oz. cooked green lentils
4 oz tinned white haricot beans (mashed a little)
A medium onion chopped and fried in olive oil
2 oz brown bread crumbs. 1 large egg, and plenty of pepper and a little salt.

'After mixing well I shaped them and fried them in a little olive oil. My vegetarian daughter and I thought they were very tasty. We had them with a small side salad as a supper dish. Definitely worth making.'

Fried Vegetable Marrow

Take a vegetable marrow. Peel it and take out the seeds.
Cut into quarters and boil until tender.
Take them out to drain and cool.
Make a mixture of parsley and thyme and bread crumbs and pepper.
Egg over them with a paint brush, dip them in the bread crumb mixture and fry in lucan oil. Place in the oven to drain and dry.

Marilyn Smith, Chair of Cheddleton WI: 'The fried marrow was quite good. My mother used to cook marrow like this - along with some other vegetables and salad we enjoyed it. Our tastes are different today.'

Eds: 'Lucan oil was a vegetable oil used for frying. Olive, sunflower or any vegetable oil could be substituted. Cookery books of the time abound with recipes for vegetable marrow, many of them sweet.'

Many of the older people we spoke to remember marrow and ginger jam and marrow chutney. Marion can remember having delicious ginger jam like this made by her grandmother during the Second World War. Pam said her mother was still making it in the 1970s Marilyn Smith got this recipe for marrow and ginger jam from her mother aged 88.

Marrow and Ginger Jam

1 large marrow - ripe. 1 lb of sugar to each pound of marrow peeled
Sliced quarter oz of whole ginger to each lb of marrow.
Peel the marrow and remove the seeds. Slice thinly.
Weigh it and place alternate layers of marrow and sugar on a large dish.
Leave till the next day.
Put in a preserving pan, add the ginger in a muslin bag and boil gently until the juice is syrupy.
Remove the ginger and pour into warm dry jars and cover at once.

A variation on this uses the juice and rind of 2 lemons instead of ginger.

Tapioca Cream (Cold)

1 breakfast cup full large pearl tapioca and 1 of cream.
Boil the tapioca thoroughly, whip the cream to a froth or until it drops off the spoon. Mix the 2 together and flavour with lemon or vanilla.
Sweeten to taste.

Eds. 'An unusual recipe. In Mrs Beeton and Eliza Acton tapioca is eaten as a hot pudding. Grated lemon rind added to it during cooking gave it a very good flavour. We tried it as well and followed the instructions on the packet for quantities and added the cream when it was cold. Wickedly fattening, delicious with poached plums. Definitely worth making.'

Marilyn Smith: 'Oh boy! it took us back to our school days when we used to call it frog spawn. Not too bad really if you could tackle the texture.'

Food Memories in Wetley Rocks

After Cheddleton we took the road that Susanna and her sister would have taken out of the village towards Wetley Rocks when they walked to the village school to teach sewing to the little girls. Wetley Rocks was once noted in all the tourist books for the strange formation of rocks along one side of the main road - a 'must see' of the day. On past the church and village school we went until, on the outskirts of the village, we came to Wetley Abbey Residential Home where we talked to some of the ladies.

Mrs Dorothy Milner (nee Walters) aged 97

Dorothy was born in Cookshill in 1904 and has lived in and around the area all her life. She was one of nine children, all breast-fed, who were born and raised on a farm which kept pigs, cows and poultry. Although only five acres in total it enabled the family to be self-supporting and derive an income from it. It also gave employment to a couple of farm labourers. They had no clocks, relying on sundials - truly another age - but Dorothy has adapted well to the 21st century!

She remembers porridge without milk and sugar, and bacon and eggs from the farm for breakfast. They ate well at a time when some of the people living and working in the towns did not, the farm supplying all the

Wetley Abbey

milk and meat that they needed and they grew their own fruit and vegetables. Sunday dinner was a huge joint of home-killed meat followed by a rice or barley pudding and sometimes cooked fruit, or a pudding boiled in a cloth. Barley pudding was her great favourite. The barley was boiled in water until tender, then milk - whole milk - and sugar was added and it was baked in the oven. *"Much better than rice pudding!" "The only things we bought in any bulk was flour and coal. The men would go to the wharf and bring bags of slack back for the kitchen range - a mixture of good and poor coal. Sometimes they bought some oatcakes back with them as well or biscuits as a treat. At Christmas we had a big chicken, and then later on a turkey."*

Like Connie's mother, at Basford Hurst, Dorothy's mother made all their butter and cheese from the farm milk, all their cakes and bread, and, for the winter, she bottled fruit, salted beans in large earthenware pots and put down eggs in isinglass. She must have been indefatigable, for into the bargain she paid scant attention to the 1876 and 1880 education acts that stated that all children under 13 had to go to school. Dorothy did not go to school until she was 10 - her mother taught her children at home, where they also helped on the farm. Dorothy's lively intelligence and questioning mind still bears testimony to the quality of her education and upbringing.

The family must have been hardworking and blessed with good business acumen. They became involved with the canals and with poultry farming on an ever increasing scale. Her uncle built Foxearth Hall and her sons are still engaged in the poultry farming business and bring home-produced milk, eggs and fruit to her in the home as she is distrustful of modern foods and robust in her condemnation of them: *"It was a good life. We had real food, fresh food, proper food. Modern milk is rubbish - no goodness in it at all - full of disease and chemicals."* With BSE, and with food poisoning at an all time high, one feels there is justification for her feelings.

Milking in Staffordshire, early 20th century.

Susanna: Marriage and Edinburgh

In April 1860, after a very short engagement, Susanna married the Reverend Charles Ingleby, who had seen her at church when she was living up at Sharpcliffe with her sister and younger brothers. Before they married they made plans to move into the house that Charles shared with his mother at Oakamoor. Neither Susanna or Charles's mother were happy with the arrangement so it did not bode well from the start.

A Victorian engraving showing a clegyman and his family at Christmas.

The Reverend Charles Ingleby.

Oakamoor nowadays is a quiet village set in a deeply wooded valley. It was not so in 1860. A huge brass foundry, Thomas Bolton's, filled the valley polluting the air with acrid smoke, and noise, which must have added to the torment of the few weeks that Susanna spent there.

What should have been the start of many years of happiness ended after eight short weeks in the complete breakdown of her marriage. Susanna fled by train from her marital home while her husband and mother-in-law were away, and was literally rescued by her father and whisked away to stay with her sister Penelope in Edinburgh while he tried to sort out some sort of financial settlement for her. He could not afford to support her, so getting money for her was crucial. One thing was certain in those days - she would never marry again.

Smoky Oakamoor in the early 19th century.

Oakamoor, showing the canal and railway from Cheddleton.

The details of her terrible ordeal on her honeymoon and afterwards at Oakamoor can be read in our book *Finding Susanna*. As she was so very unhappy there, and at Oakamoor for such a short time, we have not asked anyone there to try out her recipes for us.

Susanna's sister, Penelope, had married well - into the wealthy Brodie family in Scotland - and had a lovely country home as well as a town house in the best part of Edinburgh. Susanna stayed with her for several weeks, enjoying, as best as she could in the circumstances, the company of her young nephews and nieces, away from Staffordshire where everyone, she guessed, would be talking about about her failed marriage.

Penelope Brodie

Mrs Sheila Lewis of Edinburgh kindly tried out two of Susanna's recipes and also found photos for us of Penelope's houses, where Susanna stayed.

Recipes

Canary Pudding

3 eggs, the weight of 2 eggs in sugar, ditto butter, the same of flour.
Beat the butter to a cream, add the sugar then the flour then the well beaten eggs. Boil for 1½ hours. Flavouring lemon. Serve with a wine sauce.

Sheila: 'The pudding looked as if it might be rather solid - in fact it was quite light. I made a wine sauce, using the recipe given to me, with a combination of blackberry & rhubarb jam which was extremely nice. Much appreciated by my son. The pudding was put into a buttered basin and the top covered in non-stick baking paper.'

Eds. 'Definitely worth making. In Susanna's time a floured pudding cloth would have been used. Anything used must be tied on very tightly to stop water getting into the pudding and make sure the saucepan doesn't boil dry. The flavouring would be grated lemon peel and the juice of a lemon.'

Wine Sauce

A quarter pint of water. 1 glass of sherry.
1 tablespoon of jam. 1 tablespoon castor sugar. Lemon juice.
Put the water and the sugar into a pan and simmer for about 10 minutes.
Add the other ingredients. bring to the boil, strain and serve.

Eds. 'Susanna did not have a recipe for wine sauce although the pudding recipe called for it. This is from Mrs Beeton's 1859 edition and is the one we gave to Sheila Lewis. We tried it substituting red wine for sherry which gave a sharper sauce which was delicious. Definitely worth making.'

Almond Pudding

3 eggs well beaten. 3 spoonfuls of flour.
Mix them well together and as much milk as will fill a pint basin.
White sugar to your taste
7 or 8 bitter almonds blanched and pounded.
Do not put these in until the last minute as they are apt to sink.
Boil it three quarters of an hour and serve with a wine sauce.

Sheila - 'I tried this on myself and a friend. I found that bitter almonds are very difficult to come by so I used one and a half tablespoons of ground almonds and a quarter of a teaspoon of almond essence. I made the pudding as directed in a pint basin but it rose - a bigger basin is needed!

It was very pallid in appearance and the almond flavour not strong enough - perhaps bitter almonds are stronger, certainly if I did it again I'd triple the amount of almond essence. I made an apricot wine sauce to go with it which was very nice. My friend and I managed two helpings each.

I got interested in bitter almonds and looked up Mrs Beeton (1859 edition). She said that:

'bitter almonds are injurious to animal life on account of the great quantity of hydrocyanic acid they contain, consequently it is seldom used in domestic economy. If used to give flavour it should be used with great caution. A single drop of essential oil of bitter almonds is sufficient to destroy a bird and four drops have caused the death of a middle-sized dog.'

However, she still went on to include bitter almonds in her recipes though I noticed that later editions substituted vanilla essence in the same puddings. I also read in *The Cooks Encyclopaedia* that bitter almonds are illegal in the USA. In fact making these two puddings has led me on many searches, finding out many new things and new places, quite close to where I live, which I've never noticed before! Perhaps Agatha Christie had read Mrs Beeton on the dangers of bitter almonds. Certainly they figure as a reliable and lethal poison in her books!'

Penelope Brodie's Baberton House.

Three
ARMITAGE

Susanna

The end of summer came. It was time for Susanna to leave her sister Penelope's homes in Scotland and go back to Staffordshire to face real life. She returned to Cheddleton and lived at Woodlands with her sister Emily Jane. She was bruised by her experience and very reluctant to go out into the community. To be separated from your husband in her time was socially very embarrassing - however justified the cause - and she knew that she could now never remarry and have children of her own. However, her father obtained a settlement from Charles Ingleby so Susanna was at least financially independent. She lived quietly and perhaps would have done so for the rest of her life had not another tragedy befallen the family and altered her life yet again.

Her brother - still estranged from their father - had married in 1861 and in 1862 was overjoyed when his wife had a son. Sadly the joy was short lived. Like so many Victorian women his wife became desperately ill with puerperal fever - common then because of the lack of hygiene at childbirth - and almost always fatal. After a few short painful weeks she died and John William wrote to Susanna and begged her to come to live

Armitage church

with him and care for him and his baby son Ralph. Though the death of her sister-in-law was a tragedy, for Susanna it was a chance of a worthwhile life, caring for a child and running a home - almost as if she had been married. She hurried to her brother. She was to stay with him and Ralph for the rest of her life.

John William had rented a house in Armitage to take his wife and baby son to - but it was Susanna who went to Armitage with him in 1862 and stayed there until 1870. They were probably the happiest eight years of her life.

John William, Susanna and Ralph taken in 1868.

Armitage then had a population of almost 1000. It was not a pretty village, straggling towards nearby Handsacre and dominated by the huge pottery works which manufactured, as it still does, sanitary ware. The cottage John William had rented was fairly small and Susanna had little help - a maid and a nursemaid, someone who came in to do the washing, and seasonal help in the large garden. Entertaining on any scale was impossible. But she was happy. She and John William threw themselves in to village life and made many friends.

The village had a baker, two butchers, a draper, three shoemakers, three general stores and a tailor - but it was to nearby Rugely that Susanna went for her main shopping. Rugely was a bustling industrial town of over 4,500 people with every shop she could have possibly wanted. It had all the usual food shops and wine and spirit merchants, chemists and bookshops, but also three dressmakers, a milliners, two watch and clockmakers, a photographer, a stationer, haberdashers, confectioners and a 'fancy repository'.

She worshipped at Armitage Church. We met Bridget Boyd who now lives in the Old Rectory, and through her the present rector and his wife, and they were able to test some of Susanna's recipes for us. We chose to give them mainly biscuits and cakes as Susanna's house was not large enough for formal dinner parties, though her friends did call for afternoon tea. A memorable tea-party took place in Armitage in 1863 which Susanna recorded in her diary:

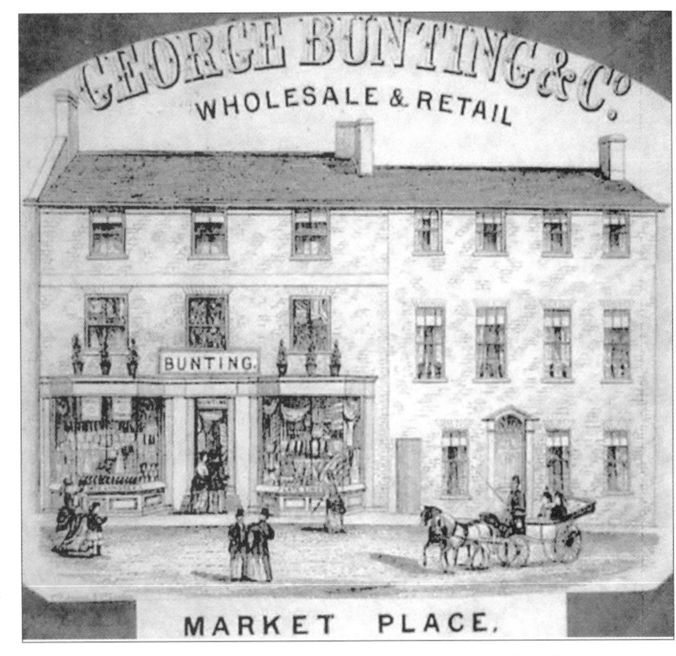

A Rugeley shop - from Susanna's scrapbook.

'March 10th
The Prince of Wales was married to Princess Alexandra Caroline Maria at Windsor. There were great rejoicings everywhere. Mr Spode gave more than 120 men roast beef and plum pudding in a tent in his park, and afterwards tea to about 70 women. Mrs Wilson and Mrs Birch gave tea to about 160 children and rosettes were given to all.

A Victorian tea party, about 1869. Susanna owned a St Bernard dog like this one later in her life. They were very fashionable.

Mrs Wilson was the vicar's wife, and both she and Mrs Birch were friends of Susanna. Mr Spode was Josiah Spode IV, a very wealthy man. He lived at Hawkesyard Hall which his mother had bought in 1830. Bridget Boyd has asked people in the village to search high and low to see if any of the rosettes still remain, but none have been found.

Recipes

Bridget Boyd also made two cakes for us. Neither of these recipes are in Susanna's book, but they are to be found in almost every Victorian cookery book and we feel sure Susanna would have cooked both.

Pound Cake

8 oz butter, 10 oz flour, 8 oz sugar, 8 oz currants, 2 oz mixed peel, 1 oz sweet almonds, 3 eggs, milk and, if liked, a little mace.

Shred the peel thinly and blanch and chop the almonds finely.
Sieve the flour and add the peel, currants and almonds to it.
Put the butter into a clean bowl and beat to a fine cream with the hand, then add the sugar and give it another good beating.
Add the eggs one at a time, beating after each addition.
Add the flour and fruit and mix thoroughly adding a little milk to make a soft consistency if necessary. A glass of wine can be added but the cake is already quite rich. Heat the oven.
Grease and line a cake tin on both sides and bottom and bake for 1½ hrs.

Bridget: 'This was an easy cake to make and it took exactly 1½ hours to cook on gas mark 4. It looked very appetising - brown and shiny on the top and the fruit evenly distributed inside. I used an 8 inch cake tin and cooked it on a shelf slightly below centre. A moist cake, it cut well and did not go crumbly. I did not put in the wine. The family enjoyed it.'

Eds: 'Definitely worth making.'

Vicarage Cake

1½ pounds of flour, 8 oz moist sugar, a little grated ginger and nutmeg.
2 eggs well beaten, a spoonful of yeast.
Brandy. 4 oz butter and ½ pint of milk, 12 oz currants.
Melt the butter in the milk.
Make a light paste with the rest of the ingredients.
Put it before the fire for an hour to rise.
Add the currants. Stir well and cook in a brisk oven.

Bridget: 'Not a success. A strange cake to make. Stirring and mixing was hard going so I resorted to my mixer. It produced a very stiff and sticky dough. I put it to rise but it just sat there sullenly! In the oven it rose well.

I covered the top with greaseproof paper but despite this the currants ended up on the top like black bullets though the cake was nicely brown in-between them. I ended up with a very heavy dry cake. Even generously buttering a slice did little to improve it. I'd have done better to have drunk the brandy!'

Eds: 'What a shame. Poor Bridget!'

Three members of the Armitage Mother's Union cooked biscuits for us and the present vicar of Armitage, the Reverend David Thomas, and his wife Georgina, kindly held a tea party in their new vicarage. Susanna would have felt at home there we were sure as the afternoon started with prayers and a reading. Then, in their colourful lounge, tea was served and the ladies, and the Reverend Thomas, started the tasting in earnest.

The Old Rectory, Armitage, where the Rev Wilson and his wife lived in 1862. It was newly built when Susanna moved to Armitage. She often took afternoon tea there.

Banbury Cakes

Press well together 1 lb currants, nicely cleaned, 4 oz beef suet, 3 oz candied orange and lemon peel nicely minced, a few grains of salt, a full quarter oz cinnamon and nutmeg, 4 oz macaroons or ratafia biscuits rolled to a powder.
Make a rich paste [pastry] with 14 oz butter to 1 lb of flour.
Roll out one half very thin.
Spread the currant mixture over it evenly.
Roll out the other half thinly.
Dampen the edges and place on top.
Mark the whole with the back of a knife into rectangles 2 inches wide and 3 inches long.

Eugenie Simpson

Bake in a well heated oven for 25 to 30 minutes.
Divide into cakes whilst still warm.
Cooked by Eugenie Simpson

Eugenie - 'I made these twice before they satisfied me and found them difficult - especially rolling out the pastry which was so short. I solved this when I remembered a tip I had heard on the radio and rolled out the pastry on a sheet of cling film. It worked brilliantly, but I wonder what they used to use before cling film? I baked them for 10 minutes in an oven gas mark 6/7. They were better the second time as the currants were moister.'

Eds: 'Everyone enjoyed them immensely. A great success. Definitely worth making.'

Pauline Meggy

Wholemeal Cakes

8 oz wholemeal flour, 8 oz oatmeal, 1 oz butter, 1 pint boiling water.
Rub the butter into the flour and oatmeal.
Mix in quickly with a wooden spoon 1 pint of boiling water.
Make into 10 balls and press onto a greased baking sheet.
Bake in a hot oven for 10 minutes.
Cut and butter for tea.

Cooked by Pauline Meggy just before we had tea so they were still hot.
Pauline - 'I tried them out before today and found that they were better if I used less liquid, 16 fluid ounces

instead of 20. I baked them in a very hot oven, 220c, for about 10 minutes. Best eaten hot.'

Eds: 'Delicious. We had them spread with butter and home-made jam - there were very few left. Definitely worth making - and very easy.'

Ginger Bread Cakes Dora Bamford

The original recipe for these was given to Susanna by her favourite niece, Dora Bamford. Susanna was her godmother.

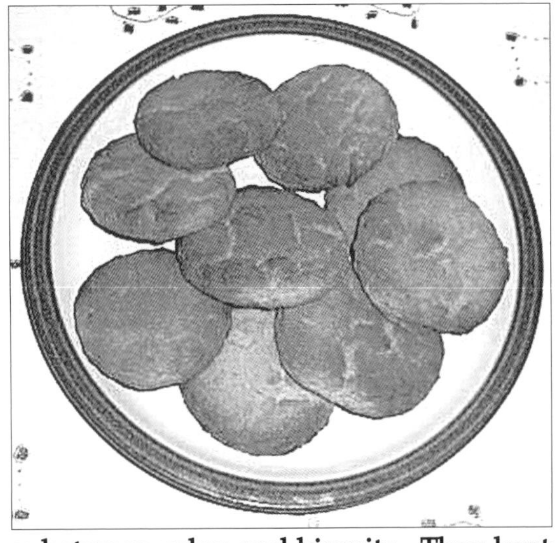

1 lb flour, 8 oz sugar, 8 oz treacle, 4 oz butter, melted, 1 oz best ginger.
Mix all together well and knead it well and cut it into thin cakes.
Bake in a moderate oven.

Cooked by Pauline Greenhough

Pauline: 'Although there was no raising agent in these they rose slightly and were like a cross between cakes and biscuits. They kept well in a tin. I rolled them out, even though the recipe does not state this, about a quarter of an inch thick and baked them at 180 c for 10 minutes. I did them twice as I didn't like them the first time - hard on top and soft underneath. The next time I used 3 tablespoons of golden syrup instead of treacle and 3 level teaspoons of ground ginger. Very good then. Easy to make.'

Eds. 'Everyone thought they were delicious. Definitely worth making.'

It was a very happy afternoon and the Vicar thanked all the ladies who had cooked. He said it was one of the nicest Mother's Union Meetings he could remember!

We felt that the ladies of Armitage had helped us capture just a flavour of the tea parties of Susanna's time and we had thoroughly enjoyed sampling the delicious cakes and biscuits. The picture on the next page is Susanna's own simple sketch of her kitchen at Armitage Cottage - sadly it was demolished in the 1930s.

Susanna's drawing of her kitchen in Armitage.

Food Memories in Armitage

Mrs Sharratt (nee Smith) aged 96

Mrs Sharratt was born, raised and married in Armitage. Her father was an estate labourer at Hawkesyard and helped to build the Priory there by barrowing bricks.

"Dad had an allotment so we never bought anything from the greengrocer. Mum did all our baking and cooking. I remember a donkey cart that used to be sent to the railway station on a Friday to collect fish for the Priory.

This tea party reminds me of something that happened when I was about 13. I'd gone into service for a doctor's family in Wednesbury. It was hard being away from home at first and one day when they were going to visit friends near Armitage they asked if I would like to go with them to spend an hour or two with my family.

They dropped me off but when they got to their friends they were out so they came back for me a lot earlier than we expected. My mother asked them in. She got out her best embroidered tea cloth and china and gave them bread and butter and some home-made jam, but as she hadn't expected visitors there was no fresh cake. Quick as a flash she sent me to get the christmas pudding that she had put away - we always kept one from one Christmas to the next, the brandy in them made them get better and better - turned it upside down and sprinkled it with icing sugar. They said it was the best fruit cake they had ever had!"

Pam with Mrs Sharratt and Mrs Wallis.

Mrs Wallis, aged 84

Mrs Wallis was born in Derby and moved to Armitage when she married. Hers was a comfortable childhood in a well run home in a village just outside Derby.

"I remember as a child that Thursday was baking day. All the bread and cakes were baked at home and I remember seeing my mother mix the bread dough in a large earthenware bowl and setting it to rise on a chair in front of the kitchen range - the bowl covered with a snow-white cloth.

Everything had to be covered in those days as there was a lot of dust from the coal fire, and our kitchen was usually full of flies and insects, so all food had to be protected. My mother and grandmother made muslin covers for the milk jugs and basins of food - sewing beads all round the edges.

On baking day mother would open the dampers of the oven and get it really hot to bake the bread. She also made cakes and gingerbread and baked them while the bread was rising.

We were given 1d a week pocket money. There were four of us - quite a small family at that time. My husband was the next eldest in a family of nine children. There were no 'school dinners' at the village school and we went home for dinner from 12 till 1 pm. Mother had to work hard to get a meal ready and on the table by the time we got home - it was always meat or fish and 2 vegetables - and always a pudding.

Our garden was quite large and we grew enough vegetables to last through the year. Mother bottled our fruit, made jam, sweet pickle and chutney. She also made raspberry and blackberry vinegar for winter colds and sore throats. Our runner beans were salted down for the winter and there would be winter cabbage and brussels sprouts in the garden. Our hens' eggs were preserved in isinglass for the winter, when they didn't lay.

Granelli's from Macclesfield who pulled their ice-cream cart by pony to Rudyard Lake.

I remember the ice-cream man used to come around the village on a Saturday morning driving a small horse and cart with a frill round the top of the cart. He wore a white apron and straw boater type hat and called out 'Creams' to attract our attention - but he need not have bothered, we'd waited for hours for his little cart to appear. We had penny cornets and licked every last scrap off our fingers so as not to waste any.

We were allowed to buy ice-cream with our pocket money from mother's birthday in May till father's birthday in September - then we bought sweets at the corner shop the rest of the year. The little plump lady who owned the shop was very patient while we decided which sweets we would buy. She would weigh them on the shiny brass scales with weights, and put them into cone-shaped paper bags.

Sometimes we bought 'lucky' packets. These were greaseproof paper bags which contained a few cheap sweets and perhaps a wire ring with a coloured glass stone in it wrapped in paper. At other times we bought a 'turnover' which was a

Tea in the garden, from a photograph taken in about 1900

pink and white pasty made of some sweetmeat. Inside you would find a cheap trinket wrapped in paper. It was always exciting to open it up and see what was inside. We also bought 'locusts' and 'tiger nuts' sometimes - revolting looking things. The Locusts had the appearance of dried up banana skins and tasted strangely sweet when chewed - they were seed pods. The Tiger Nuts looked like shrivelled pea nuts and they too tasted very sweet.

My Grandmother was a typical Victorian lady and, like Queen Victoria, loved having meals outside when the weather permitted. A table in the garden would be laid with a snow white damask cloth and napkins and gleaming silver and glass. There was no 'let-up' when taking meals outside and grace was said as usual. The glass jugs of home-made lemonade had to be covered with muslin covers to keep out the flies and flying insects which were everywhere.

Sometimes Granny would take us out for a picnic to a place where sparkling spring water gushed out of a rock. She would pack a wicker hamper with a feast of mutton pies, boiled ham, tongue and hard-boiled eggs, sandwiches and cakes of every kind. It was the time before the advent of cling film or foil wrapping so all the sandwiches had to be wrapped in damp tea towels to keep them fresh. There was no need to take anything to drink because the spring water was pure and icy cold. We took our shoes and socks off and waded in the water, splashing and playing until we were tired out. Then there would be the trek home with dragging tired feet carrying the empty hamper between us.

Sometimes we went shopping in town with Mother. First we would go to the corn stores and order the flour and the food for the animals. Also meal for our pet duck and maize for the hens which we called Indian Corn. This would be delivered later by the dray man who drove the big heavy vehicle drawn by four large shire horses."

Susanna would have recognised this account. She too went to the corn stores in Leek when she returned to Basford, taking little Ralph with her, to buy maize for their chickens and pet duck - and she too called it Indian Corn. Mrs Wallis continued: *"Then we went to the High Class Grocery Store in the High Street to order the groceries - which would also be delivered to the house - this time in a van with one horse.*

A delivery man in Hanley, Stoke-on-Trent around 1900

I was fascinated by shops of any kind but this grocery store was something special. The lady assistants were pretty and I thought they looked like my china doll. They wore black dresses with white collars and white aprons. A chair was always set for mother to sit down whilst she placed her order. I was fascinated by everything especially the overhead money rail. Mother would pay the assistant and the money would be placed with the bill in a metal container and put on the wire rail overhead. It then shot off at great speed around the shop to the office which was situated some out of the way place. Presently it came flying back, bumping round corners to stop dead over the assistant who would take it down and give mother her change and the bill. I was always sorry to leave and made up my mind one day to work there - but of course I never did."

Gingerbread Cakes, page 59.

Banbury Cakes, page 57.

Pound Cake, page 56.

Shrewsbury Cakes, page 88.

Cheese Faggots, page 84.

Wholemeal Cakes, page 58.

Ginger Pop, page 32.
Seen here with Caraway Seed Buns - see Very Good Seed Cake, page 122.

Canary Pudding, page 51.

When we cooked this we lined the basin with oranges before adding the mixture - then we cooked it as the recipe. It was delicious.

Treacle Pudding, page 108.

Serve this with lashings of golden syrup and single cream - it is almost unbeatable on a cold day.

Gateaux des Pommes, page 75.

Stewed Pears, page 89.

Pea Soup, page 92.

We cheated by using a large tin of mushy peas instead of dried peas - and we used a blender! The result was a lovely warming winter soup with very little effort. This is the one made by Carolyn.

Rissoles, page 111.

Lentil Cutlets, page 125.
John and Sue Sneyd had theirs cold, but we tried them hot with a leek and mushroom sauce - they were very tasty.

Corn Oysters, page 44. We ate them cold with a side salad.

Four
ABBOTS BROMLEY

Susanna

Susanna's eight happy years in Armitage were about to end. In 1870 Susanna, John William and her little nephew, whom she affectionately called 'Ralphy', left Armitage and moved to Abbots Bromley about 5 miles away. It must have been a wrench for them as they had made many friends in Armitage, but the cottage they had rented was small and very damp. There was a terrible smell under the floors which was so bad that sometimes they had to move upstairs, and they did not seem to be able to overcome the problem. In Abbots Bromley they rented a much bigger and more modern house, Lea Fields, a little outside the village. It was quiet and overlooked fields.

Abbots Bromley is, and always has been, a very different village from Armitage. There was no heavy industry in Abbots Bromley, no canal bringing clay for the pottery works and coal for the kilns. It was much, much quieter - farming was the main livelihood. Many of the houses were half-timbered. It was, and is, a pretty village with a Butter Cross marking the site of the ancient market, granted by charter in 1227, although the first written mention of the village goes back even further. In 943 the manor was called 'Bromleige' and was given to Wulfsige the Black. Near the Butter Cross is a house called The Crofts. It used to be called Bull Stake House, the once popular sport of bull-baiting taking place outside.

The village did not have a 'great house' or lord of the manor; its allegiance was to the Abbey at Burton, and over the years the village became increasingly prosperous. After the dissolution of the monasteries the lands were given to Sir William Paget and the village became known as Paget's Bromley. During the 18th and early 19th centuries the family gradually sold the lands and the village reverted to its old name of Abbots Bromley. Just outside Abbots Bromley there is a grand house, Blithfield, home of the Bagot family, and Susanna was on visiting terms with Lady Bagot.

The most famous thing about Abbots Bromley is its Horn Dance, thought to date back to 1226 and celebrating St Bartholomew's day. By the time Susanna encountered the custom, it had become little more than a source of revenue for the dancers - all men - who donned the ancient horns

The Abbots Bromley horn dancers.

which still hang in the church and went from house to house dancing for money. Susanna did not approve and wrote to Ralphy that, *'it used to go to Charity but they keep all the money for themselves now'.*

The dance still takes place every year at the beginning of September, organised by two local families who have had this responsibility for many years. The dancers collect the ancient horns, some of which are thought to be reindeer horns and over 900 years old, from the church, and dance with them through the village starting at just before 8 am, stopping at predetermined places throughout the village, and finishing at 8 pm when the horns are returned to the church for safekeeping and a short service is held.

Shortly after Susanna and John William moved to Abbots Bromley Ralph was sent away to school, but he came home for his holidays and during one of these, in December 1873, Susanna took him to a soup kitchen, which she had helped to organise with other ladies in the village, to alleviate the suffering of farm labourers. For many years there had been poor harvests. Farmers laid off staff and there was real hunger and hardship amongst the labouring classes.

Schoolchildren of Abbots Bromley near the Butter Cross c. 1900.

The gentry families of the village clubbed together and bought a large cauldron to boil up a huge quantity of nourishing soup - 30 gallons a day - housing it, we think, in the barn of one of the farm houses near the village centre (next to the fire station in Goose Lane) owned then by a widow, Mrs Grace Ward. They subsidised the cost of the soup to the tune of about £25 a week between them (in today's money) and organised a rota to serve it to the poor who needed it - charging them 1d a pint (about 19p).

There were seven ladies involved. It was served once a week, every week, starting in November 1873, and continued for 5 months. All the ladies on the committee helped, even Lady Bagot, and even some of the men came to help their wives serve the soup. This was a genuine community effort to help those least able to help themselves and Ralph was taken to see what it was like to be poor.

Susanna recorded each serving of the soup in her diary. The entry for December 5th 1873 is typical:

'I went to church in the morning. At 3 o'clock I went to the soup kitchen. Lady Bagot and Mr & Mrs Pickering and Katie (their daughter) were there. About 24 gallons of soup were sold.'

Recipes

Year 4 children at The Richard Clarke First School, Abbots Bromley, who study local history as part of their curriculum, made the soup for us. A special 'soup day' was organised by their head teacher, Pam Potter, and we are most grateful to her for her enthusiasm and support and for all the work that the staff, parents and children at the school put in. It really brought history to life. The morning was spent in preparation under the careful supervision of their class teacher, Emma Watson, and other staff who came in to help, especially Sue Martin and Hilda Bennett.

This picture shows Emma with two of her pupils slicing up parsnips.

The Uttoxeter and Abbots Bromley Soup

As was provided for the poor people in 1873. 30 galls, that is 240 pints for one day. The poor people paid 1d a pint, and it costs 1½d. The gentry gave 10s a day and their time.

28 lbs beef 6 pecks potatoes
3 lbs rice 2 lbs flour
6 packets of pea flour
Carrots, turnips and onions
Celery tops, pepper and salt.

Pupils chopping celery and potatoes.

The children peeled and chopped parsnips, carrots, onions and celery tops. A few did not know what parsnips were and most had not prepared raw vegetables before. The beef was cut up very finely by a member of staff in the school kitchen. The pea flour was a problem as it is now not available, so dried peas were added instead. A member of staff added the water to the raw ingredients in a huge saucepan and it was gently boiled for 2 hours, and stirred from time to time.

To go with the soup the children also made oatcakes. Susanna had a recipe in her book from a Mrs Miller, who lived in Abbots Bromley.

Oat Cakes

First make a batter (the same thickness as used for batter puddings) of milk, about the heat of fresh milk from the cow, and oatmeal and a little flour and a few eggs.

The quantities and method are vague. We used 8 oz oatmeal, 8 oz flour to 1/2 pint of milk and 1 egg. This worked well. Mrs Miller's sound like the traditional Staffordshire oatcakes, which are more like pancakes but the

Mixing the oatcakes.

children (closely supervised) made them rather drier.

Children: 'It was a very messy mixture and didn't stick together very well. We had to squash it together with our hands and flatten it to make biscuit shapes. We baked them for about 15 minutes in a moderate oven. '

Eds. 'Both soup and oatcakes were thought delicious by all. One little boy summed the soup up very well, *"T'ain't 'arf filling,"* he said. Both definitely worth making in the winter.'

The children had been studying Victorian life during the week and while waiting for the soup to be ready some read history books, some made place setting cards for the guests the head teacher, Mrs Potter, had invited. Others hoovered the floor, cleared up and set the table. Wild flowers from the hedges round the school field were arranged as table decorations. Everyone helped to set the scene.

Shaping the oatcakes.

During the lunch hour the children changed into the clothes their parents had prepared for them, as did all the members of staff. Soon the guests arrived, including the present Lady Bagot, and they sat at the table, whilst Marion, dressed as Mrs Susanna Ingleby,

Children and adults queueing for soup in Walsall during the miners' strike of 1926.

"Sit up straight!'

Year 4 girls waiting for their soup

spoke to the children. She had of course already immediately separated them into girls, on one side of the room, and boys on the other as they came in! They had to 'sit up straight', and were told 'don't fidget' as the famine conditions they would have endured, if they had been alive then, were described to them. The children threw themselves into the spirit of a school in the 1870s! The soup was brought in and, after the guests had been served of course, the children queued for their cup of soup and an oat cake.

Just as Susanna had taken her little nephew Ralph to see the soup being made in order that he might learn what it was like to be poor, so the children of Richard Clarke school had made and eaten their own soup and tried to imagine life in their village over 130 years ago. It was a wonderful learning day for us all.

ABBOTS BROMLEY GREAT PUDDING EVENT

Some weeks later the ladies of Abbots Bromley got together, just as they had in Susanna's time. This time it was to make five of her puddings for us and have a public tasting in the lovely old Church House.

Space was limited and soon all the 40 tickets allocated were gone. We noticed that there were several gentlemen in the room to try the puddings. Everyone had a piece of paper and was asked to comment and vote on each pudding, although they were only given a number not the name of the pudding until the end.

Orange Delight

Pare 5 or 6 oranges and cut them into thin slices.
Pour a cup of sugar over them.
Boil 1 pint of milk and whilst boiling add the yolks of 3 eggs and 1 tablespoon of corn starch which you have rubbed smooth in a little milk. You must stir every moment until it begins to thicken like custard, then pour it over the oranges.
Beat the whites of the eggs to a froth and add a tablespoon of sugar and put this on the custard. Set in the oven to brown.

Cooked by Mrs Rosalind Rushworth

Rosalind: 'I added the eggs to luke warm milk and then very gently heated the mixture to thicken it. It was nice and I would make it again but I would add orange liqueur to 'pep' it up.'

Eds. 'This was rather like a lemon meringue pie without the pastry. The method given, of adding the eggs to boiling milk, seems very odd - you'd expect to end up with scrambled eggs!'

Tasters: Most people found it too runny and many said it was too bland - the oranges too sweet together with the custard and meringue. Some liked it though. It looked very pretty.

Oz Pudding **Dora Bamford**

3 oz bread crumbs, half a pint of milk boiled and poured over the crumbs, 3 oz butter, 3 oz sugar, 2 eggs, a wine glass of wine.
Beat all together and bake for 20 minutes.

Cooked by Louise Hayward who was a cook for many years for the children at the Richard Clarke First School, and Annette Knight, who helped her organise the pudding event.

Louise: 'A fairly foolproof pudding, a bit like bread and butter pudding but very, very sweet. I think it needs less sugar. It took 60 minutes at 180c, but double the mixture took 2 and a half hours. I wondered whether that was because I used a pyrex dish which conducts heat differently from the old pottery ones that Susanna would have used. Quite nice cold.'

Annette: 'I used a little less butter and served it hot. The family liked it.'

Tasters: (It was served hot) It was either loved or hated. 'The flavour of the wine was quite strong.' 'Very easy to eat - a winter pudding'.

Eds. 'We noticed that most of the men present had two helpings! Worth making.'

Annette Knight, Hilda Bennett and Susan Ball.

Gateau des Pommes *The Queen Magazine*

Slice 8 large apples.

Add 6 oz sugar, the juice of a lemon and the rind grated.

3 eggs well whisked, half an oz isinglass or gelatine dissolved in a small quantity of water. Mix all together.

Set on the fire until quite warm but do not let it boil.

Pour it into a mould. This will fill a pint mould.

Cooked by Hilda Bennett and Mrs M Harvey.

Hilda: 'The first time I made it it was not very nice - the apples were not cooked and it was a sort of mousse. Difficult to be sure how many apples to use as they vary so in size. I think it needed more lemon.'

Tasters: Most found it refreshing and light, though most agreed that it needed more lemon. 'Delicious.' 'More a lady's dish than a man's'. 'Delicious. Had a second helping. Any more?' The TOP pudding with our tasters by a long way.

Eds. 'Marion tried this but cooked the apples first adding lemon zest and used lemon jelly instead of gelatine and lemon and eggs. 1 1/4 lbs tart apples to 1 packet of jelly. She used hardly any water in the apples and melted the jelly in them whilst they were hot. 2 oz cooked apples and lemon slices decorated the dish. Cheating - but very good. Well worth making. Delicious with single cream.'

Mrs Cotton - Ralph's Grandmother

Potato Pudding ***Mrs Cotton***

8 boiled potatoes, 2 oz butter, yolks and whites of 2 eggs, quarter of a pint of cream, a dessert spoonful of white wine, a morsel of salt, the rind and juice of a lemon.

Beat all to a froth and add sugar to taste. Crust as you like. Bake it.

If wanted richer put 3 oz more of sweetmeats and almonds and another egg.

Cooked by Brenda Adams

Brenda: 'I made it without the extras and exactly as the recipe said. I baked it with a standard pastry case for 45 minutes in a hot oven and added a little more lemon rind and juice and cream - but you have to judge that depending on the size of the potatoes.'

Tasters: Most agreed that it was unlike any modern pudding but liked the variety of texture and tastes. Quite a complex pudding on the palette in spite of its humble ingredients, and quite filling.

Marion tried this. She made a very short pastry crust and put marmalade on the bottom before adding the potato mixture, taking 8 potatoes to mean 8 ozs of potatoes. This worked very well. She sprinkled almonds on the top and baked it in a hot oven for 35 minutes. It almost had the texture of a cheesecake and was delicious hot or cold with a little single cream. Her next-door neighbour, Peter Shamash, aged 81, sampled it and declared it very good indeed. He was excited by it as it reminded him immediately of a sweet cake that his Jewish grandmother made when he was a child in France at Passover. As

Peter Shamash

a strict Jew she could not use wheat flour and made a delicious light sponge cake using potato flour instead which he remembers to this day with pleasure. How smell and taste can conjure up memories.'

Corn flour on Bread and Preserve

1 tablespoon corn flour to be mixed in a little cold milk.
Pour boiling milk on this and stir up together and boil until quite thick.
Cut slices of bread which dip into preserve and water and place in a dish.
Put in an oven to brown.
Use 1/4 pot of damson jam to 1/4 pint of cold water and melt this on a fire.

Cooked by Susan Bull and Jean Biggs

Susan: 'I make my own bread and used that so it was as similar to Susanna's recipe as it could be but the bread was too dense and I think made it rather stodgy - a lighter bread would be better. Easy to make.'

Brenda: 'We had puddings like this at school! I added sugar to the corn flour custard as I felt it was too bland otherwise. You need a good flavoured jam for this.'

Tasters: All agreed this was a winter pudding and to our great surprise it came second in the best pudding vote, though not everyone liked it. 'Tastes of poverty to me' said one, 'a way of using up stale bread', another.

Eds. 'We agreed with Brenda - the quality of the jam is crucial. Pam thought it was disgusting!'

Jean Biggs, Louise Hayward and Brenda Adams

Marion with Hilda Bennett.

Memories of Food and Farming in Abbots Bromley

Philip and Susan Ball

Philip Ball is 85. He was born and brought up on a farm on the Staffordshire/Derbyshire border which had been in his family since 1653. Susan, his wife, and a Londoner, married him in 1944. Their memories recall sharply an age which now seems light years away - and indeed closer to Susanna than to us. Their vivid account must be typical of the lives of so many of the people in and around Abbots Bromley at the end of the 19th century and well into the 20th.

Philip: *"A grocer called once a month and delivered by wagon, that was in the 1920s. Meat, usually an 8 lb rump of beef, was delivered on Saturday by horse and cart, and bread once a week, 8 to 10 loaves at a time. The only meat we purchased, apart from the Sunday joint, was on market day in Uttoxeter. Then we bought brawn or polony, or pigs chawl or sausages - and as a great treat a pork pie. Cakes and biscuits were baked at home but at Christmas mother used to buy a few luxuries from the grocer. The baker sent his bill once a year and when it was paid we got a box of chocolates.*

We once sold a cow to the local butcher for £20 and agreed to have meat in lieu of payment. We had meat for 2 years! We had pies that my mother made - sparrow and rook (only the breasts, the legs were too tough) and roast rabbit which we caught ourselves. It was roasted whole with string tied round the head and through the mouth. And she always made Queen of puddings on a Sunday."

Susan: Although a Londoner when Susan married into this farming family she joined them on the family farm.

"In the 1940s we seemed to live on rabbits, bread and cheese and pickle and game. And eggs of course, and field mushrooms and very fatty bacon - all from the farm. And I remember a 'beestie' Yorkshire pudding that was made to go with the joint on Sunday. Beastly I called it to myself as it was very stodgy and horrible - but made for reasons of economy. After a cow calved it was illegal to sell the milk for 4 days so the milk was put in a shallow pan and the cream that rose to the top - the beastings - was used for puddings and custards. That was after the calf had had what it wanted of course. I tried to make butter from it but it wouldn't work.

On Rogation Sunday the vicar came at about 6.30pm and several neighbouring farmers also, and a short service was held in the yard - then they all came in for supper.

My husband's parents didn't drink - I don't think they could afford it as they had 8 children, 6 of whom survived, but they usually had 9 gallon casks of ginger beer in the cellar which the children were allowed and 9 gallon casks of a drink called hop bitters - a sort of beer I suppose. Philip says he thought it was horrible and thinks it was made annually for the gangs of Irishmen who came to help with the harvesting. He remembers the next door farmer making a sort of sparkling beer for his harvesters which was also pretty awful.

The neighbours all helped each other with haymaking and the corn harvest and it was all horses until well after the second world war. We never did more than was essential on a Sunday; the horses needed a rest anyway!

Harvesting in Staffordshire in the early 20th century.

When I first met Philip's parents I thought them both very Victorian in outlook and dress. We had no electricity or mains water or even a W.C! We milked by hand and I was amazed how primitive it all was - but I loved it, and his family.

I cooked at first on an old black range and hot water came from a side boiler which had to be filled by hand. When we got a Rayburn in 1949 and a hand pump to pump the water into it it was absolute luxury! Fuel was rationed then of course but everything we shoved into it burnt on the Rayburn - not like the old stove which sulked unless it was fed decent lumps of coal.

In 1950 we moved to another farm. My father gave us £100 as a moving present and we bought an Aga - £111- we still had no mains water or electricity but a good well, a spring and a windmill pump, with a petrol engine when the wind didn't blow. And we had a bathroom and a W.C. What more could we ask for!"

Five
IPSTONES, BELMONT and FOXT

Susanna

In 1873 another change occurred in Susanna's life. Her father, the Reverend John Sneyd, died. The rift between him and John William had never been healed and he had been less than warm towards Susanna after she had gone to live with her brother. However, both she and John William had maintained close contact with family and friends in Cheddleton and the surrounding area, and after their father's death they moved back to Basford Hall. By right, of course, as the eldest son, Ashcombe should have been John William's - but he had been disinherited. Ashcombe went to Dryden Henry Sneyd, his younger brother.

Basford Hall had been neglected and was damp, cold and in need of repair. Though it had piped water, unreliably brought up by a pump from the Bath House below Basford, it was probably every bit as uncomfortable as Susan Ball's first home in Abbots Bromley in the 20th century. But electricity, even generated by a petrol engine, would have amazed Susanna - she was still using candles and oil lamps. The house was large, she had little help, and the money that she and John William had at their disposal was not really sufficient to run it properly.

The bathhouse 'tower' can be seen at the left end of the picture.

For the first few months after their return all was cordiality and warmth within the family - then gradually the brothers started to quarrel. Bickering about land boundaries escalated into court cases which dragged on for years. Ralph was growing up. He was still away at school and we know from Susanna's letters that he was becoming wilful and difficult to deal with. John William was a blunt country gentleman and could find little to relate to in his aesthetic and artistic son. He grew increasingly irritated by him. Between warring brothers, and warring father and son, poor Susanna was 'piggy in the middle'. She threw herself into church life at Ipstones, her father's old parish.

IPSTONES

Susanna's father had been the vicar of Ipstones for almost 30 years and when they returned to Basford, in 1874, Susanna worshipped at St Leonard's church, making the long uphill walk from her home at Basford when the weather allowed. She always sent flowers to decorate the little weathered local pink stone church at harvest festival, even if she could not get there. She helped to make a carpet for the chancel when the church was renovated in1877 and she paid for a window, which still shines above

Ipstones St Leonard's

the altar, to the memory of her father. Memorials to her mother and other members of her family also still stand on the window sills.

In Susanna's day Ipstones was a very different village from the one we see today. There was more industry; canal and mineworkers filled the village. They earned good wages and spent them recklessly - mainly on drink. Her father had called it, when he went there, *'a hard and irreligious place'*, and had set about bringing religion and schooling to the village with energy and enthusiasm - and he had an impact.

There were lots of shops in Ipstones then; three butchers, five grocers, one of whom was also the local monument engraver, and four boot and clog makers, as well as a tailor and numerous beer shops.

Ipstones High Street

Ipstones nowadays is a charming, quiet, somewhat sleepy village on first sight - but this is deceptive. Village life is still vigorous and thriving with a strong sense of community and a modern well-used village hall built for our Queen's Silver Jubilee. The church still plays an important part in village life and there is a thriving historical society. Apart from a butcher's shop it has a 'Trading Post' where everything from fresh bread, wines, spirits, groceries and newspapers can be bought and neighbours meet for a gossip in the coffee shop.

Recipes

When we set about testing the recipes, the ladies of Ipstones church and the Cheddleton WI worked with the same cooperative spirit that Susanna had so obviously enjoyed. They held a 'tasting' morning together in the church, to sample the biscuit and pudding recipes they had cooked.

Cheese Faggots *C.A. Sneyd-Kynnersley*

2 oz cheese grated, 2 oz butter rubbed into 2 oz flour.
Add a little cayenne pepper.
Mix with a little water to make a paste.
Cut into pieces a quarter inch by 4 inches.
Make some into rings to push the others through when they are baked.
Send to the table hot.

Cooked by Hilary Jack

Hilary: I would call these cheese straws. In her instructions, Caroline Anne omitted to add that the pastry should be rolled out thinly before cutting or to give the cooking temperature. I cooked them in a hot oven, gas mark 7, 220 C for about

Caroline Anne Sneyd-Kynnersley, Susanna's cousin

12 to 15 minutes and used a hard cheddar cheese.

Hilary Jack

Tasters: 'Delicious', 'More-ish', 'light and crisp,' 'Were they called faggots because they were like bundles of sticks?'

Eds. 'Everyone thought that the 'faggots' were delicious, and so pretty in the unusual way they were presented - lovely for a buffet party or at Christmas. Definitely worth making.'

Ruth Flint

Ginger Biscuits

From Eliza Acton's Modern Cookery, which Susanna had in her library.

3 oz of good butter with 2 lbs of flour. Add 3 oz sugar and 2 oz of powdered ginger.
Mix with a little new milk and knead into a stiff paste.
Roll out very thin and stamp out with a cutter.
Bake in a slow oven until they are crisp but keep them a pale colour.
A couple of eggs can be mixed with them but it is of no material improvement.
An extra oz. of sugar can be added if a sweeter biscuit is liked.

Cooked by Ruth Flint

Ruth: 'Determined not to be beaten, I had seven attempts to make satisfactory ginger biscuits and broke a wooden spatula! In the end I came to the conclusion that for modern tastes 2 lbs of flour to 3 oz of butter made them much too hard. I discovered that 8 oz of flour and more sugar made nice biscuits but doubt whether they were worth making!'

Tasters: 'Thumbs down all round.' 'Too dry, too hard.'
Ruth Flint: 'Much too gingery.'
Eds. 'Such a shame after Ruth's valiant efforts. She gets a gold medal for perseverance!'
The ginger biscuits that the Armitage ladies made were lovely. We suggest you stick to those - on page 59.

Biscuits *Dora Bamford*

Take 1 lb of flour, 6 oz sugar, 6 oz of butter or dripping, a small quantity of salt and ginger.
Rub well together in the hands until it becomes powdery.
Then mix it with a spoonful of milk and 2 tablespoons of beer.
Roll it out very thin and cut it out with a glass and bake in a quick oven.

Dora Bamford
Susanna's favourite niece

Violet Randall

Cooked by Violet Randall

Violet: 'Easy to make.'

Tasters: 'Bit Dry', 'Lovely, not too sweet not too dry', 'Crisp but not hard - nice', 'More-ish', 'Bland - better than no biscuit!'

Eds. 'No real enthusiasm for these.'

Excellent Biscuits *Marianne Sneyd-Kynnersley*

Melt 12 oz butter in a pint of new milk and pour it upon 12 oz loaf sugar.

When cold put in half a teaspoon of yeast and a whole one of caraway seeds and flour sufficient to make a stiff paste.

Roll out very thin, prick, and cut with a tin.

Cooked by Barbara Fishburn

Marianne Sneyd- Kynnersley, a cousin

Barbara: No cooking instructions are given but I guessed they would be similar to other biscuits - that is a brisk oven, say gas mark 6, about 10 minutes. The recipe made a large quantity of biscuits. They kept very well in a tin. After 2 weeks the taste remained unchanged but they were no longer like roof tiles! Perhaps they liked hard biscuits in Susanna's day.

Tasters: 'Could do with a bit more sugar.' 'Tasty.' 'Georgina, aged 2, liked these.' 'Smooth tasty and with lots of flavour.' 'Bland. I wouldn't come back for a second one.'

Shrewsbury Cakes ***Marianne Sneyd-Kynnersley***
Beat 8 oz butter to a fine cream and put in the same weight of flour.
1 egg beaten, 6 oz sifted loaf sugar, half an oz caraway seeds.
Mix all together and roll them thin and cut them round with a glass and prick them all over and lay on sheets of tin.

Shrewsbury Cakes

Cooked by Hazel Bradbury

Hazel: 'Marianne gives no cooking temperature but I baked them for about 30 minutes on gas mark 4. I sprinkled sugar on some of them.'

Tasters: 'Delicious, the winner.' 'Very nice.' 'Excellent.' 'Acquired taste.' 'Delicious, I shall bake these.'

Hazel Bradbury

Eds. 'We decided to try these ourselves. Rolling out was a problem as the dough was very soft and sticky. It was solved by cutting the dough into cubes of about 3 cms, and then rolling these in floured hands and patting them into shape on the baking tray. We used baking parchment instead of a greased tin tray. Definitely worth making.'

In Susanna's day the now familiar packets of biscuits were not available. Gingerbread biscuits could be bought at the bakers but most women made their own biscuits. The general conclusion reached was that nowadays, with so many excellent packet biscuits available, it is probably not worth the effort. However, we think that the *Shrewsbury Cakes* and the *Gingerbread cakes* tested at Armitage are exceptions, both excellent and not like any packaged biscuits now on sale - and both are free of the 'flavour enhancers' and colourings now found in most of our foods.

Stewed Pears and Swiss Cream

6 large pears cut in two lengthways, peel them slightly.
Put them in a very clean stew-pan, cover over with 3 oz white sugar, powdered slightly.
Cut the rind from a lemon and cut into thin strips, and press the juice on top of the sugar. gently shake the pan to dissolve the sugar.
Put on a very slow fire for 10 to 15 minutes, shake it gently once or twice.
Turn the pears gently with a fork and cook again for another 10 to 15 minutes.
When done put on a dish to cool.
Arrange on a serving dish and pour the syrup over.
They may also be done in a slow oven.
2 teaspoonfuls of currant jelly, or jam, or marmalade may be mixed with the syrup, or half a glass of maraschino or brandy.

Swiss Cream ***Miss Aston***
Take a pint of cream and boil it 10 minutes
with the grated rind of a lemon and sugar to taste.
Put a dessert spoon of fine flour into the juice of
a larger lemon and mix well
together, then pour the boiling cream upon it stirring until it thickens.
A few macaroons in a dish with preserve are a great improvement.

Cooked by Jean Hodgetts, Jo Donlan and Sheila Leeson.

Jean: 'I used Sheila's home made jam in the swiss cream and cornflour instead of ordinary flour which was too 'floury'.'

Tasters: Pears: 'Absolutely delicious - I liked the lemon in the pears. I'll definitely make both the pears and the swiss cream.' 'Light refreshing and delicious.' 'Very nice, lemon added a nice tang.' 'Delicious, fresh tasting.'

Swiss Cream: 'Like trifle.' 'A bit floury.' 'Lovely, like cheesecake.' 'Nice sweet. I would enjoy it after Sunday tea.'

Jean Hodgetts, Jo Donlan and Sheila Leeson

Some of the other ladies who attended the tasting morning, hard at work recording their opinions.

Eds. 'There is no doubt at all that the pears were the outright winner with all the tasters.'

We were interested in the last comment of the tasters. We have been lucky enough to have been invited for 'tea' at various homes in the North Staffordshire area. It is not 'tea' as Marion thinks of it coming from London where it is a paltry affair of a 'cuppa' and a piece of cake or a few biscuits, but like those that Pam, from Yorkshire, remembers from her childhood. They were substantial meals and her mother-in-law expects to be given just such a meal now. The 'trifle' or swiss cream would go down a treat! You could use sponge fingers instead of macaroons.

The urns on the window sill behind the ladies (tasting photograph opposite) are all Sneyd memorials. An unusual Sneyd family tree made of slate with enamel discs on it can still be seen in the tower of the church.

In 1877 the church was renovated and Susanna joined with her sister, Emily Jane, niece Dora, and other local ladies to make a carpet to go in front of the altar in the chancel. They had instruction from Mrs Wardle, later Lady Wardle, of the Leek Embroidery Society. Sadly the carpet is no longer there but we were able to piece together the story of the way it was made from Susanna's diaries, with help from Barbara Fishburn - and the story can be read in a little booklet *Susanna's Carpet?* available from the vicar, the Reverend C.M. Scargill (all proceeds go to church restoration).

Surviving fragment of Susanna's carpet.

Susanna would almost certainly have known the great grandfather of our next cook - Carolyn Leebetter from Cheshire. William Willmer was churchwarden at Ipstones 1886-1922 and headmaster of the village school in Ipstones 1884-1911. Carolyn has been tracing her family history. Her mother was born in the village and married in St Leonard's church.

Carolyn has visited Ipstones recently and she loves the village. She cooked two dishes for us, Sea Pie and Pea Soup.

Sea Pie

Brown carrots, turnips and onions in 2 oz boiling fat.
1½ lbs bullocks steaks.
Sprinkle flour over.
Make a suet paste of 1 lb flour 8 oz suet.
½ teaspoon baking powder, ½ pint water.
Put the meat at the bottom of the saucepan and the paste at the top.
To boil one hour after the paste is put on.

Carolyn: 'The instructions were not clear so I followed a similar recipe from a Mrs Beeton that I had, adding the vegetables, then the meat, and cooking them slowly covered for an hour. I put the suet crust on and cooked it for another 1½ hours as I wanted it to be really tender. The family were impressed and really enjoyed it.'

Eds. 'This is what sailors used to do on sailing ships - using ships biscuits crumbled on top of the stew - hence the name 'Sea Pie' even though it has no fish in it.'

Pea Soup

Put a pint of old peas in cold water a quart over night and 2 quarts more to be added.
Add 2 carrots scraped and sliced thin, 1 turnip peeled thick, 2 small onions, celery and parsnip, herbs in a bouquet.

Carolyn Leebetter

Boil for a good while and then rub through a sieve.
Add 2 tablespoons of flour which has been mixed in a little of the soup, this keeps the vegetables from sinking to the bottom.
Add a little ketchup and browning, 2 oz butter or a little dripping and boil up again.

Carolyn: 'I used dried peas and did exactly as Susanna instructed. The worst job was rubbing it through the sieve - hard work. I was very tempted to use my blender but I didn't give in! I boiled it for 3 hours, then made a roux with the butter and flour and a little milk before adding it to the soup. Fresh mint from the garden improved the flavour no end - it was a bit bland until then. My husband enjoyed it.'

Eds. 'It is interesting that Susanna adds neither pepper or salt - we would use both. The ketchup she used for flavouring was probably homemade and might have been mushroom or walnut, though both were available commercially by the 1880s.'

Rev. Goodacre, other clergy and church wardens, including Carolyn Leebetter's great-grandfather, with members of the church choir, taken in about 1910 outside St Leonards.

BELMONT

Not far above Basford Hall is Belmont Hall - a grand house built by Susanna's great-grandfather. He planted extensive woodlands round the house - he was given a gold medal by the Royal Horticultural Society for his planting in the late 1790s. The trees are now fully mature and the very beautiful and deeply wooded valley round the hall is a permanent memorial to him, although the house has been substantially altered now and part of it knocked down.

Belmont Hall

Being not too distant Susanna often used walk up to Belmont to call and see her favourite aunt, Aunt Mary, who was living there in the 1880s.

The stables of the old hall have now been turned into a lovely house which overlooks the remains of the hall's kitchen garden and old green houses. Mrs Jodi Peck lives in Belmont Grange, as it is called, with her husband John, and cooked Belmont Cake for us. Aunt Mary, no doubt, often had the cook make it and perhaps Susanna had a slice when she called in for tea.

Jodi is Canadian by birth but has thrown herself into English village life and has made strenuous efforts to raise money to restore the slate and enamel Sneyd memorial in Ipstones Church. For this photo she wore her mother's antique silk blouse and set the table for tea with an embroidered cloth given to her as a wedding present. We are sure Susanna would have approved.

Belmont Cakes - enough for two cakes ***Marianne Sneyd-Kynnersley***
1 lb of flour, half a pound of dripping, half a pound of currants, half a pound of raisins, and half a pound of sugar.
1 teaspoonful of baking powder and one of soda.
Add two eggs and butter milk to mix.

Jodi: 'No instructions were given, but I looked in contemporary cookery books and in most of them the dripping was rubbed into the flour then the other dry ingredients added. Finally the beaten egg and as much liquid as was needed to make a moist but not runny mixture was added. The cakes would have been baked in a moderate oven for about an hour. I found them rather dry but I think I cooked them for too long. They were much better eaten warm as when they got cold the dripping seemed to set very hard. A good flavour, they kept well.'

Eds: 'Barbara Fishburn of Ipstones also cooked this cake for us and we had it at a local history day which we held in Ipstones village hall. It was a moist fruit cake and very much enjoyed.'

FOXT

The little village of Foxt is about 3½ miles by road S.E. of Ipstones, though it is less than this on the footpath across the fields. When the Reverend John Sneyd, Susanna's father, was vicar of Ipstones he canvassed all his friends and relatives to support him in building a church there and dug deep into his own pocket as well.

Foxt Church - built by Susanna's father in 1839.

Christine Chester

In 1838 the church was opened and the Rev. John Sneyd used to walk from Ipstones to Foxt most Sundays, no matter the weather, to take a service there. The population of Foxt was about 120 in 1871 but there were several shops - a butcher, a shopkeeper who was also a farmer, and 2 beer houses - the owner of one also being a carter and timber merchant. Today there is one general shop owned by Neville Brindley, who also runs a mobile grocery van around many of the neighbouring villages, and there is one fine pub, the Fox and Goose.

Mrs Christine Chester, a farmer in Foxt for many years and a keen local historian - who has recently helped produce a new book on the village (*20th Century Foxt!*) - tried two traditional recipes for us which benefited from the long slow cooking she was able to give them on her farmhouse Aga.

Figgy Pudding **Mrs Barstow**

8 oz figs cut small, 6 oz sugar, 6 oz suet, 6 oz bread crumbs, 2 to 4 eggs, 1 tea cup of milk.
Boil in a mould for 4 hours and serve with a wine sauce.
Half quantities for a smaller pudding.

Christine: 'I'm used to making boiled puddings and treated this the same way - made sure it was watertight on top and that it didn't boil dry. Although it was very light and crumbly it was very, very sweet, and, for

us, far too greasy - I had indigestion for days! I think the amount of suet could be greatly reduced.'

Eds. 'The ratio of fat to flour or bread crumbs in other cookery books of the time varies quite considerably. A few have an even higher ratio but many have less, about 6 oz suet to 8 oz bread crumbs or flour is probably better.'

If you want to go the whole hog try this recipe from Ancient Greece, which Eliza Acton quotes in one of her books:

'Heroditus's pudding'

1 lb of minced raisins, 1 lb of suet, 8 oz of bread crumbs
4 figs, chopped small, 2 tablespoons honey
2 glasses of sweet wine and the grated rind of a large lemon
Boil for 14 hours.

Eds: 'We have not tried it and Christine thought she would be ill for a week if she did!'

North Staffordshire Fermity **Mrs Bloor**

Steep a small quantity of fresh wheat (by placing it in a covered jar overnight with some water in a very slow oven).
Boil this in milk, slightly thicken with flour and add sugar to your taste.

Christine: 'In all honesty porridge is a more pleasing alternative to my taste.'

We are grateful to Christine for trying this for us. Mrs Bloor was Susanna's cook at Basford for a good many years. Mr Bloor had been the gardener and when he died we think that Susanna took Mrs Bloor on partly out of charity, as thereafter the accounts book show an awful lot of crockery being broken, bottles of whiskey being bought for Mrs Bloor, and notes in her diary that Mrs Bloor would get 'very cross' if any instruction was given to her.

However, Mrs Bloor was very kind to Ralph and did many things for him. Ralphy had a passion for collecting things - it was a passion which lasted all his life. Susanna and Mrs Bloor did their best to look after his collection whilst he was away at school. In a letter to him Susanna wrote:

Ralphy

My Dear Ralphy,
'Mrs Bloor has cut the bad bits off the slow worms for you and put them in jars with acid. They look very well.............'

Perhaps Mrs Bloor cooked fermity as a *'wholesome breakfast'* for Ralphy when he was a child. He was about eight in this picture. Eliza Acton recommended a wheat based *'porridge'* which she calls *'wheaten-grits'*, as it *'aids stubborn constipation'* and is better than oatmeal which has a tendency *'to heat the blood'*.

Gloucestershire W.I. has this recipe in its 1935 year book.

Furmity
1 quart of milk, 4 oz raisins, 4 oz currants, 3 tablespoons flour,
1 cup of prepared wheat.
Put the wheat, currants and raisins into the milk
and let it come to the boil.
Thicken it with flour then add 1/4 of a nutmeg grated
and sweeten to taste.
Boil 10 minutes and stir well or it will burn.

Eds. 'This sounds more like a rice pudding than porridge and much more interesting than Mrs Bloor's - though by 'prepare the wheat' we imagine that it still required the overnight steeping and cooking in a very slow oven. How times have changed - even since 1935. Nowadays some children don't even get 'instant' porridge before they set off to school.'

Food Memories in Ipstones

Before we leave the Ipstones area here are some memories that Ruth Flint has gathered from elderly residents for us.

Alan Taylor aged 77

Alan is originally from Ball Haye, a village when he was young but now part of Leek. Alan was one of 5 children - but they also had an uncle and his grandma living with them, and a dog who was treated as one of the family, even to having the same meals off a plate. His father worked shifts in a textile mill, 6 pm to 8 am. Although they were poor Alan never went hungry - his mother was a wonderful and economical cook.

On Sunday they had huge joint which was then used cold and rehashed in some way or other until Thursday.

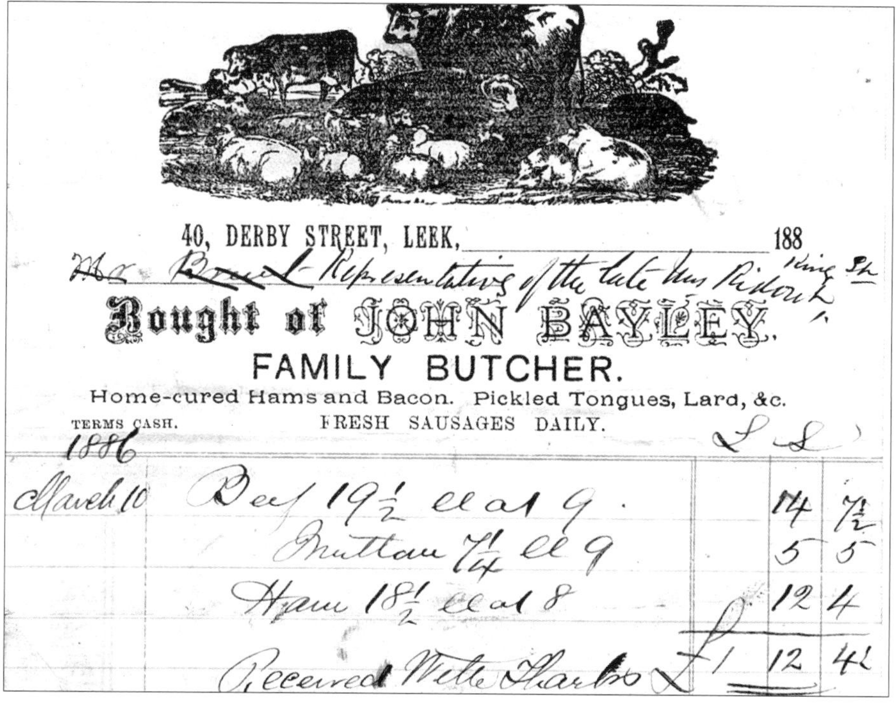

40, DERBY STREET, LEEK, __________ 188

Mr Representative of the late Mrs Ridout King St

Bought of JOHN BAYLEY.

FAMILY BUTCHER.

Home-cured Hams and Bacon. Pickled Tongues, Lard, &c.

TERMS CASH. FRESH SAUSAGES DAILY.

1886		£	s	d
March 10	Beef 19½ lb at 9		14	7½
	Mutton 7¼ lb 9		5	5
	Ham 18½ lb at 8		12	4
	Received With Thanks	£1	12	4½

Saturdays they had meat and potato pie which was cooked in a huge washing up bowl. Savoury ducks (a sort of faggot) were bought from the butcher. A bowl was taken to him early in the day and then collected later with the 'ducks' and hot gravy. Offal was bought from a lady specialising in it - cooked cow's udders which were sliced like ham, boiled sheep's head, brains, boiled in a saucepan and eaten on toast, hearts, tripe and onions cooked in milk in the oven, and pig's trotters. Supper was at about 9 pm and was often potato and onion done in a frying pan - one of his favourites.

His father grew all their vegetables but as he seemed permanently tired Alan helped and gradually took over.

His mother made them treats as well as cooking her own bread and cakes. Toffee apples and slab toffee were made occasionally and left over pastry pieces were covered in butter, then sugar, then rolled up and cut into slices and cooked as biscuits. *'Delicious,'* says Alan.

Chicken only appeared at Christmas and in the winter his mother made all her own mincemeat, ginger wine, Christmas puddings and Christmas cake. He remembers his father iced it when he lost his job at the mill and was at home.

Groceries were ordered from the Co-op once a week and were delivered by horse and cart, the 'Divi' (dividend) being saved to buy shoes. On November 5th they made a guy and had a few sparklers and his father bought 2d worth of paraffin to make sure that the bonfire lit even if it was a wet night. But no food. Alan's childhood was a happy time in a loving home - no luxuries though!

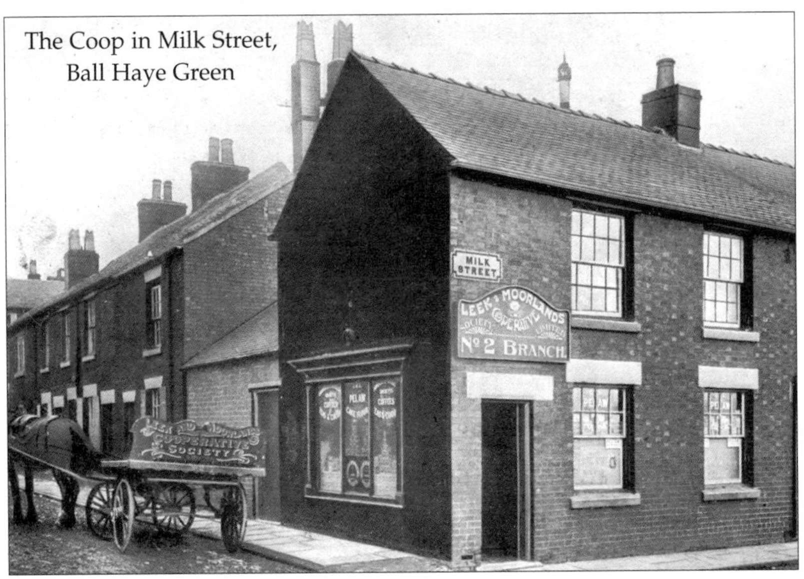

The Coop in Milk Street, Ball Haye Green

Ruth spoke to a great many old people. All remembered offal as being an important part of their diet - tripe, cow's udders, brains on toast, sweetbreads, pigs trotters and sheep heads. Almost all had a joint only once a week which was then 'stretched' for as many days as possible.

We were intrigued by the cows' udders. We had heard of all the other types of offal that had been mentioned but udders were new to us. We rushed to our old cookery books. In a recipe of 1394 there was a description of a dish being like 'the substance of ham and made of uddery.'

In his diary for 1660 Samuel Pepys wrote: *Oct. 11th - Mr Creed and I went to The Leg in King Street where he and I and my Will had a good udder to dinner.* And then in a cookery book dated 1857 we found a recipe:

To Roast Tongue and Udder

After cleaning the tongue well salt it with common salt and saltpetre three days; then boil it and likewise a fine young udder with some fat to it (but separately from the tongue) till both are tolerably tender; let them become cold; then tie the thick part of one to the thin part of the other, and roast them together. Serve with a good gravy and currant sauce. A few cloves should be stuck in the udder. This is an excellent dish.

Even if we could find anyone to sell us an udder we decided that cooking this was one 19th century experiment too far!

Breakfast, for most of the old people Ruth spoke to, was most often porridge or bread and dripping - and teatime was again, for the children, usually bread and dripping. 'Lobby' was mentioned again. One lady, Margery Gilson, age 88, said she so loved it that she used to say to her mother that if she was going to die she wanted lobby just before she did!

All remembered boiled puddings - jam roly-poly with custard, spotted dick - a suet pudding with currants or raisins - and apple dumplings. One man, Bill Bradbury, age 91, recalled 'dummy' - a boiled suet pudding with no fruit or jam in it. When asked if this wasn't very boring he replied, *'There was six of us children, we weren't really worried as long as it was something to eat.'*

Others recalled that there was always a big saucepan of soup simmering on the stove and that they were allowed as much of that as they liked if they were hungry.

Apples appeared frequently in all sorts of puddings. Thelma Head, age 77, remembered Apple Charlotte which her mother used to make. *"It was a layer of bread in a dish with sugar sprinkled over it, followed by sliced apple and sugar and then alternate layers of apple and bread until it was full, finishing with bread, and then milk poured over it and baked until the top was brown and crispy - delicious."* Marion tried it. I used brown bread and think white would give a better result. Pam says, *"My mother made this regularly and so did I when my kids were little. I prefer it to apple-pie."*

Thelma also remembered another dish - 'pobs'. Pobs was another name - like lobby - that we had not come across before. Back to the books and dictionaries. Mrs Gaskell was familiar with 'pobs'. In *Mary Barton* the nurse says, *'the child were awake and crying for its pobbies.'* The dictionary informed us that Pobs is a nursery name for porridge. So it may have been, but for Thelma and her family it was a concoction of onions, milk, lots of salt and pepper and bread which her parents often had for their supper.

Most people had their main meal of the day at midday, meat of some sort and two vegetables and a pudding - usually boiled - or rice, or tapioca, with only bread and butter or bread and dripping for children before they went to bed.

A donkey water carrier and, below, the picture of a donkey carrying wares, by Susanna.

Treats were often home-made but errands could be run and a 1d earned to spend on sweets or even an ice cream. Many recalled the ice-cream man coming round the villages his cart drawn by a donkey. One old man said, *'we used to wait for him to come up to Ipstones. His donkey was so pretty with red, green and yellow ribbons in his mane and the man would ring his bell and we'd run out. Cornets for a half penny and lovely they were too.'* Susanna drew this donkey carrying wares for Ralphy - we found it in one of his scrap books.

There were other street traders whom people remembered visiting Ipstones: a greengrocer with a horse and cart; a handcart delivering finnan haddock (smoked) from Grimsby via Leek, and coal by the bag or load. It was cheaper by the load so the children had to race out if they heard the coal man coming as it was first come first served. Knife sharpeners with their wheeled grinding carts came, and salt by the block was brought round. This was taken home and kept in a pot by the fire. Some remember it being their job to crush it up - often using a potato masher. Gypsies brought clothes props and pegs to the door.

A pedlar at the door.

Listening to these memories we were struck by how nutritious the diet was. Adulteration of flour and milk by dishonest traders - rife in Susanna's day - was a thing of the past by the time these people were children. Perhaps the people Ruth spoke to were lucky and had mothers who could make the very most of what there was. But the vegetables were fresh and largely home grown, cakes and a lot of the bread was homemade and even though there was a lot of fat in the diet there were a lot of vegetables and carbohydrates as well.

Factory girls in nearby Stoke on Trent

It may not have been exotic or exciting but it was a balanced diet - and of course as children they all had plenty of exercise before the age of the car and television. Children walked to and from school, usually four trips a day as they came home midday for dinner. Street games were played after school in the vehicle-less streets - each season having its own games which all children knew. The sight of an overweight child then was a rarity.

Leek Station and below, Derby Street, one of Leek's main thoroughfares, c 1890.

Six
LEEK

Susanna

Once back at Basford, Leek was the only town that Susanna visited regularly. She had many friends and acquaintances there whom she visited when she went into town shopping - calling in for tea or lunch. She almost always took the train into Leek and then walked home.

On our first visit to Staffordshire we went from Cheddleton to Leek and understood at once why she took the train into town and walked back. It is uphill all the way into Leek but down hill coming back!

Apart from social calls, Susanna attended meetings, classes and lectures in the newly opened Nicholson Institute to which she and John William, amongst many others, had contributed financially. A First Aid course was amongst them, and she was proud of the certificate she was awarded.

The Nicholson Institute

Leek was a very prosperous and important town in Susanna's time. It was a silk town, noisy, dirty and bustling, with a population in excess of 11,000. One of the many silk mills was run by Sir Thomas Wardle, knighted for perfecting important new silk dying processes which enabled raw silk to be produced in vibrant colours. He also worked closely with William Morris for several years, re-establishing the natural dyes that were such an important part of Morris's designs.

There was a thriving cultural life. National figures such as Oscar Wilde and William Morris came to Leek to give lectures - usually in the

8, STOCKWELL STREET,

Leek, April 19 1888

Mr Smith

Bought of JOHN FALLON & CO.,

Fish, Fruit, Game and Poultry Salesman,

OYSTER MERCHANTS, &c.

		£	s	d
March	a/c rendered	6	16	3
10	oysters 1 Score		2	6
19	oysters 1 Score		2	6
23	do 1 do		2	6
23	Shrimps			6
"	plaice fileted			7½
"	finnies 1 3/4 lbs			5
April		7	5	3
10	Sole 1 lbs 1/4		1	4
"	finnies			5
"	Sole 1 1/4 1/4		1	8
14	oysters 1 Score		2	6
"	Rhubarb 2 lbs			6
"	oranges		1	

Nicholson Institute. Leek was no sleepy backwater! Susanna attended some of these and also went to several given by Ralph when he regaled the good citizens of Leek with talks about his travels. He distributed drawings and pamphlets showing his 'curiosities'. Susanna funded his foreign travels to collect specimens and she even helped him to write his speeches.

And she often called on her trusted lawyer, Mr Joseph Challinor, to seek his advice in dealing with the troubles that beset her and her family.

The shops in Leek were legion: 37 general traders, 23 boot and shoemakers and 2 'cloggers', 19 grocers, 14 drapers, 14 tailors, 13 dress makers and milliners, 11 bakers, 9 tobacconists, 8 butchers, 6 provision dealers, 3 chemists, 3 confectioners, 4 watch and clockmakers, booksellers, newsagents, printers, tea dealers, umbrella menders, photographers, hairdressers, cabinet makers, coal merchants, auctioneers and wine and spirit merchants - and a huge number of public houses and beersellers.

The cookery classes she attended were run by a Miss Scoles - though we don't know where they were held - and one of the books that Susanna might have used was *The Scholar's Handbook of Household Management and Cookery* by W.B. Tegetmeier. It was published in 1876 and written especially for such classes. This picture shows a children's class.

The lesson for the day chalked on the blackboard was for lemon pudding, vegetable soup and rissoles - all recipes which we found in Susanna's book. Notice that there are no boys in this class - boys were not expected to know how to cook, it was still 'women's work'!

Girls' cookery class - a board school in Longton.

Recipes

Jean Bode, wife of the well-known local historian Harold Bode, cooked two dishes that are in Susanna's personal cookery book, but we are almost certain that they were recipes which she made when she attended the cookery classes in Leek as the wording is exactly the same as in Tegetmeier's book.

Jean Bode

Macaroni Cheese

Wash 4 oz of macaroni in cold water.
Boil this in water adding salt, half an hour.
Strain off the water and boil in a pint of milk, stir to prevent burning and boil until quite soft for about 1 hour.
Have ready 2 oz grated cheese (near the rind) and a little butter and pepper and salt.

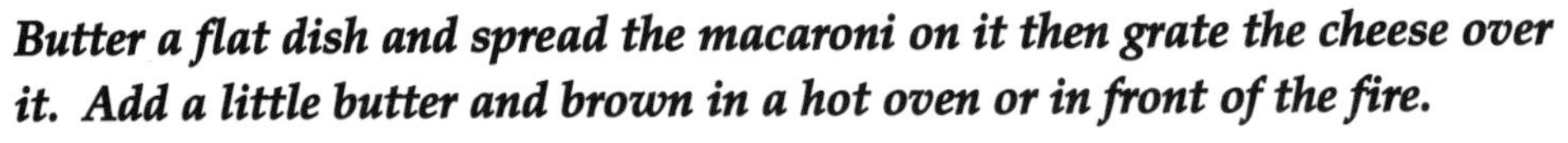

Butter a flat dish and spread the macaroni on it then grate the cheese over it. Add a little butter and brown in a hot oven or in front of the fire.

Jean: 'Filling, cheap and easy to make - good as a lunch or supper dish.'
Eds: 'Well worth making.'

Treacle Pudding

8 oz treacle, 8 oz flour, 4 oz suet, half a teaspoon baking powder, half a teaspoon ginger
1 egg, 1/4 pint of milk, a little sugar because of the lemon if that is used, or a little salt.
Dip a cloth in water and then flour it and tie the pudding in it and boil 2 1/2 hours. If not time for that divide the pudding in two cloths put in boiling water and keep it boiling.

Jean: 'I made the pudding on two separate occasions - it was delicious, very light and tasty, and we enjoyed it. When I have made treacle sponge before I have always put the treacle in the bottom of the basin before adding the pudding mixture. However, this said mix them altogether, so I did. I put the mixture in a basin, covered the top then wrapped the basin in a cloth before boiling. I thought a ginger sauce might be nice with it as a change to custard. I made a white sauce in the usual way then added sugar and ginger. It went with it very well.'

Eds. 'Well worth making - a lovely winter pudding.'

Three members of Woodcroft (Leek) W.I. kindly agreed to be our next cooks. They meet in St Luke's Church, built in 1847, in Queen Street. The end of the church, where the choir used to congregate, has been screened off and is now used as a comfortable church room.

The Wardle family were closely associated with this church, especially Lady Wardle. Using the wonderful silks that were produced in her husband's factory, Lady Wardle led a group of local ladies who became the famous Leek Embroiderers. Many of their stunning altar panels can be seen in local churches and St Luke's has several of which it is justly proud.

We asked the ladies to try two of Susanna's recipes. Again we chose economical recipes from her book which may well also have come from the cookery classes as they are both ways of using up left over meat. We are most grateful to Margaret Shenton for organising this for us.

Lady Wardle's embroidery ladies.

St Luke's, one of three grand Anglican churches in Leek. There were also many non-conformist churches and a large Catholic church.

One of the ornate altar frontals in St Luke's - made by the Leek Embroiders.

Rissoles

A teaspoon of thyme and parsley warmed and rubbed.
4 oz meat chopped fine, the same of bread crumbs, a teaspoon of flour to bind and an egg.
Cold milk will do.
Make the balls of this mixture and fry them in boiling fat.
Flour the rissoles and egg them and roll in bread crumbs before frying.

Linda Wakeham

Linda Wakeham made these

Linda: 'We all enjoyed the recipe. My 14 year old son thought they were homemade burgers, though we did feel that they were rather bland. I had already added a chopped onion but they still needed a bit more flavour.'

Eds. 'Yet another case of a recipe described as 'bland' - we are so used to highly 'flavour enhanced' foods today.'

Goblet Pie *Scholars Handbook, Tegetmeier*

2 oz scraps of cold meat,
2 oz apples chopped
2 oz suet, 2 oz raisins, 2 oz currants,2 oz sugar.
Pastry crust 12 oz flour, 4 oz dripping, a teaspoon baking powder.
Make a paste (pastry) and roll out 1/4 inch thick.
Put the meat, apple and dried fruit mix into a dish and cover with the paste. Bake for 1/2 an hour.

Chris Mould cooked Goblet Pie for us.

THE SCHOLARS' HANDBOOK

OF

HOUSEHOLD MANAGEMENT AND COOKERY.

COMPILED AT THE REQUEST OF

The School Board for London.

WITH AN APPENDIX OF RECIPES USED BY THE TEACHERS OF THE NATIONAL SCHOOL OF COOKERY.

BY

W. B. TEGETMEIER,

AUTHOR OF "A MANUAL OF DOMESTIC ECONOMY."

London:
MACMILLAN AND CO.
1876.

The name is an old one. In 1688 Goblet, or Country Pie, was described as one with one with 'gobbets of flesh in' - pieces of meat.

Chris: 'I substituted sultanas for raisins and currants in the filling and used 2 oz lard and 2 oz margarine for the pastry. My left-over meat was pork. There was such a lot of pastry in proportion to the filling that I put a layer at the bottom of the dish as well as covering it - but it was still very thick. My family would have preferred a more moist filling so if I do it again I will add more apple (cooking not dessert as I did this time) and use a bigger dish. This all sounds a bit critical but in fact everyone enjoyed it once they had got over the surprise of tasting sweetness with the meat. I served it with salad.'

Preparation

Eds. 'Well worth making.' Marion: 'I decided to have a go at this pie and made mine using 4 oz dripping (from a joint of roasted lamb) and 8 oz plain flour for the pastry. 4 oz left-over lamb, 4 oz tart apples, 2 oz raisins and some gravy left over from the roasted joint, plenty of pepper and a good sprinkling of oregano and baked it at 190c for 30 mins. It was delicious. We'll definitely have this again.'

Eds: 'Probably the thick crust in the original recipe was to make the meat go further and fill up empty stomachs as cheaply as possible. It was very good indeed, though, as Chris said, unusual.'

In medieval cookery meat was often mixed with fruit and 'mincemeat' always had minced meat in it. Although this may seem an odd mixture to put in a pie, we find nothing odd about serving sweet sauces and pickles to enhance meat dishes.

The last dish that the Woodcroft ladies tried was the popular 'Bubble and Squeak' - the name given, according to the *Oxford Dictionary*, because of the sound the various ingredients make in the pan as they are being fried together. Everyone still likes bubble and squeak though nowadays it usually made without the meat. Robert Browning, the poet, wrote in 1855: *'Bubble and Squeak, Blessed Thursday - the fat of the week!'* '

Bubble and Squeak

Thin slices of cold roast beef, dripping, 1 shredded onion, cold mashed potato, cabbage sliced, salt and pepper.

Heat the dripping in the frying pan.
Put the meat in and fry quickly on both sides.
Remove and keep hot. Fry the onion until browned.
Add the potatoes and the cabbage well seasoned.
Stir until hot. Turn out onto a hot dish and place the sliced meat on top.

Cooked by Barbara Clowes.

Barbara: 'Very tasty and a good way to use up left-overs.'

Eds: 'Well worth making. Pam tried this and her photo shows the bubble and squeak on top of slices meat. I think I'd prefer it with the meat cut into thin strips and mixed into the vegetables and all fried up together.'

Food Memories in Leek

We are grateful to Jean Bode not only for cooking two dishes for us but also for introducing us to Jessie Sheldon, her husband's cousin. Mrs Sheldon is a very lively and independent 97 year old who lives alone in Leek in her immaculately kept terrace house - doing all the housework and shopping herself. We took this photo of her in the spring of 2002.

She was born in Leek in 1905. Her parents had a boot, shoe and clog shop in the centre of Leek, at 28 Market Place, where they made, sold and repaired shoes, clogs and boots. It was a three storey house and they lived above the shop and workrooms. She was the eldest of four children and she has lived and worked in Leek all her life.

"I can remember things from about the age of three. Before the outbreak

Jessie Sheldon

of the First World War breakfast, every day, was porridge, egg and bacon. On Sundays we had oat cakes - the traditional Staffordshire ones - and egg and bacon. Then rationing came and bacon was one of the things rationed, so we had porridge, boiled egg, toast and margarine - Maypole Slab Dab and black treacle or jam or sometimes 'dripping.' We used to buy the margarine from the Maypole Grocers. It was in a big slab on the counter and was cut to whatever size the customer wanted. No packaged things in those days. The assistants cut the amount you wanted from the slab with wooden 'patters' and patted the amount chosen into an oblong and wrapped it in brown grease proof paper. You could also buy a pound of 'overweight' which was cheaper.

We used to have a skipping game which we played in the street after school or in the school playground. Only girls - boys didn't skip! Maypole butter, Maypole tea, Maypole Slab Dab, Out goes she.

The 'dripping' that we had during the war wasn't real dripping but my mother's own recipe: mashed potato mixed with a little lard and Bovril or Robeline and seasoned. It looked like dripping - the rest was left to your imagination! Butter was rationed as well. We had just 8 ounces a week and this was used at weekends or for special occasions."

The 8 ounces was for all 6 of them, about the same as a standard pack of butter today. In the Second World War the ration was 4 ounces per person per week. Bacon or ham was 4 ounces per week and sugar 10 ounces. Like very many other elderly people who gave us their memories Jessie's main meal of the day was midday, at about 12.30. On Sunday they had a roasted joint with various vegetables and *"the rest of the week we had homemade soups, pea soup and the like, and stews with dumplings. My mother used to save all the water in which vegetables had been boiled as stock for soups. On Fridays we always had fish, peas, parsley sauce and mashed potatoes, and on Saturdays, sausage and cheese oatcakes.*

Our mother made wonderful puddings: rice, sago, spotted dick, Yorkshire pudding eaten as a sweet with sugar and butter, and bread and butter pudding. And always apple tart on Sundays. She cooked and baked most of our food using the kitchen range - a coal fire with an oven at one side and a water boiler at the

Leek Market at the turn of the 19th century

other side. Vegetables were brought to the boil on the fire and left to simmer on the hob, the range was black cast iron and was kept polished. We used a paste called 'Black Lead' and special black lead brushes. It was hard work. We also had a gas cooker later on which she used in hot weather or when she was cooking for a lot of people. I helped with the cooking, and peeled the potatoes, washed the dishes and laid the table.

My father had an allotment and grew our vegetables. A special treat was the first crop of broad beans eaten with fatty bacon - delicious. Our mother worked at home, machining the leather uppers to make the clogs that we sold in the shop. The farmers all wore clogs in those days - the noise in the street was tremendous.

We shopped daily for food at nearby shops. Mrs Mitchell was our grocer at no 22. We went to Spearings, no 24, for bacon. We took a jar to Bull's, a shop in Derby Street facing the market, to get treacle which was sold loose, went to Mr Osborne the butcher, also in Derby Street, for our meat and to Maypole's for the margarine.

We had no electricity in our house - only gas and oil lamps and candles. The machines that were used to sew the leather were treadle machines. As the eldest child I had the bedroom right at the top of the house. At night I climbed three flights of stairs carrying my candle or a night light - there was no other means of lighting above the second floor. I left school when I was thirteen and went to work at the Co-op Mill."

2

2, DERBY STREET, Leek, 1894

Messrs Challinor & Shaw – Leek

Bought of Bull Brothers.

GROCERS. TEA & COFFEE DEALERS & TOBACCONISTS.

1894		£	s	d
	Forward		13	6½
June 18	1 dz. Matches			2½
July 6	1 Tin Enameline			2½
" 18	3 lbs. Honey Soap			10
	Blacklead			6
" 26	6 lbs. S. Soap 1/6 1 tin Enameline 2½		1	8½
Aug. 9	3 dz. Matches 7½ Pipeclay 6		1	1½
" 15	1 " Matches			2½
" 31	1 Tin Enameline			2½
Sep. 4	6 lbs. Soft Soap		1	6
" 11	1 dz. Matches			2½
" 20	1 Tin Enameline			2½
" 24	1 tin Enameline 2½ 1 dz Matches 2½			5
Oct. 16	3 lbs. Soap 10 3 dz. Matches 7½		1	5½
	1 dz. B & M. Matches		1	–
	Forward £	1	3	4

Before we leave this chapter we want to include some more recipes - and our favourite medical historians, Dr Angela Davies and her husband, retired anaesthetist, Dr Alun Davies, who have been wonderfully helpful during our researches into the Sneyd family - endlessly answering our questions, checking medical matters for us and explaining 19th century illnesses and procedures. Alun is involved with the section of medical history at the North Staffs Medical Institute. They live in Newcastle-under-Lyme - not a place Susanna visited as far as we know, although she was related to the Sneyds at Keele Hall. Angela is a superb cook, so we asked her to try two of Susanna's meat recipes for us.

Grilled Bullock's Kidneys

Warm the grid iron rub it with fat.
Cut the kidneys into slices and dip them in salad oil or melted dripping.
Lay them on the grid iron, leave for about 10 minutes.
Turn and cook the other side.
Before cooking season with salt and pepper and dredge them with flour.
Add more flour and stir and then make a gravy.

Angela Davies

Angela: 'I bought ox kidney but added chunks of field mushrooms whilst they were cooking in a frying pan. I arranged them on toast and sprinkled them with chopped chives to serve. I also tried a similar recipe with lambs kidneys. Both were enjoyable - the ox kidney firmer and with a stronger flavour. Although the recipe does not state it the core and skin of the kidney must be removed before slicing. I would prefer a thicker sauce - one flavoured with mustard would go well.'

Eds: 'The instructions are vague but Angela consulted 19th century cookery books. *Food and Cooking in 19th Century Britain* by Maggie Black was helpful. The 1 1/4 lbs of kidneys were not coated in flour but sliced and fried to seal them in 3 tablespoons of butter. 2 oz mushrooms, a shallot, salt and pepper and 2 teasp. of sauce (bottled) and lemon juice and 1 tablespoon of flour were added. After stirring, 1/4 pint of beef stock was added and the whole lot stirred over a low heat for 5 minutes to thicken. Serve on dry toast triangles it suggested. Well worth making.'

To Stew a Loin of Mutton

After keeping the mutton for 4 or 5 days bone and skin it, season well with pepper and salt and put it in a stew pan with 1/2 pint of water and a 1/4 pint of red wine and 1 spoonful of vinegar, one anchovy and an onion stuck with cloves and a bunch of thyme and parsley and a little ketchup.

Let it stew very gently 3 or 4 hours after throwing the gravy over and when nearly done add some more ketchup if liked.

Angela: 'My butcher boned me a loin of lamb (mutton seems to be unobtainable now) and strung it. I decided to make my own ketchup from a recipe in *Farmhouse Kitchen* by Mary Norwak':

Tomato Ketchup

4 lbs ripe tomatoes, 4 large onions, 1 lb demerara sugar, 1 oz salt, 2 oz pepper corns, 1/2 oz cloves, 2 teaspoons cayenne pepper, 1 pint vinegar.

Slice the tomatoes and onions and mix with the other ingredients.

Simmer for 2 hours stirring occasionally. Rub through a fine sieve.

Return the sauce to the pan and boil for 5 minutes.

Bottle when cold.

'The quantity of cayenne pepper was excessive - half that amount would do, I am sure. The meat was very tender and absorbed the taste from the cooking liquid well but we all felt that it was a little disappointing.'

Eds. 'We tried the lamb recipe too and enjoyed it - but then we did put in quite a lot more red wine, onions and rosemary. We felt it was well worth cooking lamb this way.'

Seven
THE RALPHY CONNECTION

Susanna

Susanna cared for Ralphy (Ralph De Tunstall Sneyd) until he was 16, from the time his mother died, when he was just a few weeks old, until her own death 28 years later. Ralphy became the centre of her life. She taught him before he went to school, she nurtured his passion for collecting - helping him mount and look after specimens as a boy - then she funded his collecting trips abroad as he grew up, and helped him to manage his museum. Collecting 'curiosities' was a very Victorian passion - many of our great museums were founded at this time.

When Susanna died both John William and Ralph were devastated. The main prop and peacekeeper of their lives had gone. She had accommodated Ralph's change of religion from Anglican to Roman Catholic when he was 22 and his decision to become a vegetarian - then considered very odd indeed. The change of religion was anathema to her - she was very hurt and confused by what, in her eyes, was a very wrong and evil step. It tested her patience with him to the limit, as her letters show. She tried to understand his fascination with it and even went with him to St Giles, the Roman Catholic Church in Cheadle, to see it for herself. She could not have failed to be impressed, as we were, by the sheer brilliance of the magnificent interior.

Ralph De Tunstall Sneyd

She knew Cheadle, some 8 miles south of Cheddleton, from her childhood. Her uncle, Rear Admiral Clement Sneyd, lived near there, in Huntley Hall, and her grandfather's lawyer had lived there at Daisy Bank. Her father was a magistrate and on the vestry committee of the church in Cheadle. It was a bustling market town of 3000 people in the 1880s - it is still a busy market town although supermarkets have mainly replaced the

Cheadle High Street c.1890

St. Giles, Cheadle

many small shops, but there are still some very good butchers and we bought a splendid piece of local lamb to try Susanna's loin of lamb recipe.

When we visited St Giles's church in Cheadle, described in the guide book as 'Pugin's gem' (Pugin also designed many other buildings including parts of Alton Towers and famously the Houses of Parliament), we could see at once why a boy as artistically inclined as Ralph was drawn to it. It simply shone with warmth and decoration - there is nothing cold or austere about it.

Opposite the church is a tea shop. We went in and discovered an array of wonderful homemade cakes which we gladly sampled with our coffee. They were made for the coffee shop by Mrs Kathleen Pyatt, who has lived and worked in Cheadle for many years. She raised four sons and is now the proud grandmother of six grandchildren. She loves cooking and kindly agreed to try a very Victorian cake for us - Seed Cake.

Recipes

Another recipe of Susanna's from *The Scholars Handbook of Household Management and Cookery.*

Seed Cake

10 oz flour, 2 oz dripping, 2 oz sugar, 1 egg
Half a gill of milk, a teaspoon of caraway seeds,
a teaspoon full of baking powder
Mix the dry ingredients.
Beat the egg into the milk and mix to a stiff paste.
Bake at once in a moderate oven in a greased tin for about an hour.

Kathleen: 'The cake was very easy to make but I found it rather on the dry side. You'd need several cups of tea with it! I'd probably serve it spread with butter. Friends who sampled it commented favourably but found it not quite sweet enough. One said that her mother used to make it but scalded the seeds first - presumably to make them more juicy. We felt it needed a few more seeds.'

Kathleen Pyatt

Eds: 'Caraway seeds have been used since Egyptian times for flavouring cakes and puddings - they are also used in liqueurs such as Kummel. If you would like a richer recipe Mrs Beeton has two - one she describes as 'very good' - the other as 'common' - though even that one has more fat and sugar than the one above.'

Very good Seed Cake

12 oz butter, 6 eggs, 12 oz castor sugar,
1 lb flour, pounded mace and caraway seeds to taste.
Beat the butter and sugar to a cream
Add the eggs, well beaten, gradually to the mixture beating all the time.
Add the flour and a little milk if necessary. Put into a lined and greased tin and bake for 1½ to 2 hours in a moderate oven.

This is a much more expensive cake, and, although we have not tried it, it sounds very good indeed. Incidentally caraway seeds are said to be very good for the digestion and for avoiding flatulence!

The Gloucestershire WI one of 1935 is also richer than Susanna's seed cake:

Seed Cake

6 ozs flour, 4 ozs butter,4 ozs sugar,
2 teaspoonfuls of caraway seeds
A half teaspoon of baking powder, pinch of salt,
2 eggs, a little milk if necessary.
Bake in a moderate oven for 40 minutes.

The WI obviously felt that their members needed no instructions!

In 1894, three years after Susanna's death, Ralph De Tunstall Sneyd married Harriet Brooks of Leek. Harriet was a book-keeper; her mother and sisters worked in the silk mills; her father was a wood turner. It was a love match but the Brookses had no status. John William was outraged and threw Ralph out, repeating the pattern that his father had set. Fortunately Susanna had left Ralph a house at Onecote. Ralph set about renovating Fairview using money that she had also left, and moved in with his bride. They would live there for the rest of their lives.

Harriet Brooks

He built a chapel in the garden which would eventually house Buddhas and Egyptian artefacts amongst other things, and in the garden he placed large pieces of rock from the Giant's Causeway in Ireland and a Druid's Altar - by this time Ralph was not only a practising Roman Catholic but was also into all sorts of alternatives: Buddhism, Druidism and Theosophy. Susanna would have despaired. His relationship with his father remained strained.

Sandra Henshall, who now lives at Fairview, kindly agreed to cook apple dumplings for us.

Apple Dumplings
5 apples.
Take out the cores and fill with sugar.
8 oz flour, 1/2 a teaspoon baking powder, 4 oz dripping, to make the paste.
Roll thin and cut into squares.
Put an apple in each square and roll around in the hand until all the joins are out of sight. Brush over with egg or milk and dust with sugar.
Bake or boil for half an hour.

Sandra: 'At the butchers there was a choice of beef or pork dripping. I chose pork first and it was definitely the wrong one! The pastry was difficult to roll out thin enough with a rolling pin. The baked dumplings looked OK when they came out of the oven but fell to pieces at the first

touch. They tasted awful! The boiled ones not only looked awful they were inedible. I tried again with beef dripping. This time the pastry was easy to roll out. They looked great when I took them out of the oven and tasted great - so DON'T use pork dripping.'

Eds. 'Nowadays we would probably prefer a short crust pastry made with butter or margarine, but the dumplings make a filling and delicious pudding. Spice can be added to the sugar for an extra 'kick' in flavour, and serve with custard or cream. We suggest that you stick to the baked ones - the crispness of the pastry is a good contrast to the softness of the apple.'

Marion baked these with a modern short crust using a mixture of vegetable fat and butter and used a fairly small tart eating apple and put sugar and cinnamon in it before wrapping it in the pastry - the picture of hers is shown. Her husband pronounced them 'very good indeed.' Definitely worth making.

Nina Shenton.

Ralph and Harriet had four children - three boys and a girl. We went next to his direct descendants. Nina Shenton of Thorncliffe is the great-granddaughter of Ralph's daughter, Stella, who married a Shenton. Like her great-great grandfather Nina is a vegetarian. She tried out two vegetarian dishes for us, using the kitchen in her grandparent's bungalow at Thorncliffe, just outside Leek.

Tomatoes and Cheese

Cut the tomatoes in halves, season with herbs and pepper and spread with grated cheese and cover with bread crumbs. Sprinkle with lucan oil. Bake in a hot oven.

Nina: 'I liked these best. I used 2 big beef tomatoes, 3 oz cheddar cheese, 2 oz bread crumbs and olive oil instead of lucan oil. I put sprigs of parsley from the garden on to serve. They looked very pretty and were very tasty.'

Scalloped Eggs

Take some fine bread crumbs, pepper, parsley, melted butter & make into soft paste with milk. Half fill some scallop shells with the mixture.
Break one egg on the top of each. Dust with pepper.
Set in the oven and bake for about 8 minutes or until the egg is set.

Nina: 'The scalloped eggs were nice but the raw eggs skidded off the bread crumbs and across the work surface! Gran says that I should have made a hollow in the bread crumb mixture first. Grandad liked this recipe best.'

Eds: 'Mrs Beeton has a similar recipe but uses ramekin cases.'

Sue Sneyd is the wife of Dr John Sneyd, another of Ralph De Tunstall's grandsons. She also cooked vegetarian recipes for us - lentil cutlets and transparent pudding - a sort of custard pie. She also made Susanna's salad dressing to go with the salad they had with the cutlets. They were joined by two of their five daughters, Katharine and Lucy. Ralph would have been very pleased, we are sure.

Lentil Cutlets

Wash clean a pint of split lentils, thr ow them into a quart of boiling water to which a tablespoonful of salt has been added and a chopped onion and a teaspoonful of chopped parsley.
Boil until tender which will be about an hour stirring carefully or the bottom will burn.
Drain them, rub them through a sieve into a basin and mix a few bread crumbs with them and an ounce of butter, a pinch of dried mint, nutmeg and pepper to taste.
Beat together with 2 eggs, well beaten.
Fry the cutlets in oil or butter. Shape them into a pretty shape first.

Sue: 'I did not find it necessary to rub them through a sieve and added very few bread crumbs (about half a slice of bread). They tasted very good

John Sneyd and one of his daughters

hot and would also be handy cold in a packed lunch. I used groundnut oil for frying. I'll make them again.'

Eds. 'Very similar to the Corn Oysters the Cheddleton W.I. ladies made.'

Salad Dressing

Boil 4 eggs quite hard.

Take the yolks and beat them up with a silver fork quite fine, put in a teaspoonful of mixed mustard, a little pepper and a tablespoon of salad oil Add by degrees some good cream to the consistency of thick custard and a little salt and 3 tablespoon of vinegar. Beat well together and put in a bottle.

Sue: 'The salad dressing was delicious. I used olive oil and white wine vinegar - and beat it with a silver fork! I'll certainly make it again.'

Transparent pudding

Beat 8 eggs very well.

Put them into a saucepan with 4 oz pounded sugar 4 oz fresh butter, and a large spoonful of marmalade.

Keep it stirring on the fire until it thickens then pour into a basin to cool.

Put a rich paste into a dish and pour in the pudding.

Bake in a moderate oven.

Sue: 'I used half quantities and checked in a modern cookery book for the method for a custard pie - which essentially is what this is. MUST keep stirring all the time it is thickening. We liked this - but a bit too sweet.'

Appendix 1
Susanna's Cookery Books

The original cookery book, and a photocopy, can be see at Keele University Library in the Special Collections Dept. When Susanna died, a probate inventory was made of all her personal possessions and books. The following are the cookery and household management books she had in her collection. The inventory is wildly inaccurate, but we have checked the titles against the British Library catalogue, so, where possible, we give the correct references and (earliest) date of publication. Those marked * were untraceable.

Eliza Acton	Modem Cookery (1845)
A 'Lady' who can 'help'	How we managed without servants (1877)
Isabella Beeton	All about Cookery (1871)
Isabella Beeton	The Book of Household Management (1859)
Mary Renny	What to do with cold mutton, a book of rechauffes (1863)
Phillis Browne	A Years Cookery, Giving dishes for breakfast, luncheon and dinner for every day of the year (1890)
John Charles Buckmaster	Buckmaster's Cookery (an abridgement of some of the cookery lectures delivered at the Cookery School at the International Exhibition for 1873 and 1874) (1874)
H.M. Davy	Cookery and other practical matters for working men's wives Published for the SPCK (1867)
Georgiana Hill	How to stew, hash and curry (1869)
Mary Jervey	Marnes' Cookery book for the Millions *
Mrs Marne	Maine 's Model Cooking and Housekeeping Book*
Mrs Marne	My Lady 's help and what she taught me*
Catherine Moss	Everyday work in the household. A book for girls in domestic service (1882)
Maria Eliza Rundell	A new system of Domestic Cookery (1808)
Mrs Eliza Warren	The sixpenny economical Cookery Book (1875)
Mrs Eliza Warren	How I managed my house on £200 a year (1864)
Unknown	First lessons in the Principals of Cooking*
Unknown	How to Make Cakes*

Appendix 2: **A Price Comparison**

Commodity	**1878 price**	**equivalent price now (1998)**	**2002 Tesco price**	**Items dearer now cheaper,** same
Bacon per lb	6d, 7d, 9d	£1.16p - £1.74p	£1.54 - £2.90	dearer now
Bicarbonate of soda	3d	58p	£1.02p	dearer now
Brandy (common)	1s 7d per bottle	£3.68p	£9 - £12	dearer now
Bread - brown	2d -3d	49p average	59p - 85p	dearer now
Caraway seeds	2d - 3d per 4 ozs	49p	£2.70p	much dearer now
Cheshire cheese	7d - 8d per lb	£1.43	£1.79p	dearer now
Chicken	1s 8d - small 3s 6d - large	£3.87p £10.45p	Chicken was a luxury - no battery farming. **cheaper**	
Cocoa per lb	9d	£1.74p	£2.89p	dearer now
Coffee beans per lb	1s 8d	£3.87p	Very wide choice of type and quality now available £1.59 - £2.79. **cheaper**	
Currants per lb	4d	77p	80p	about the same
Dried peas per lb	2d - 3d	49p average	26p	**cheaper**
Dripping	Widely used in 1870s Most families saved their own. Now about 50p per 8 ozs			
Eggs per 6	6d - 1s depending on season	£1.16p - £2.32p	26p cheapest battery to £1.25 free range organic. **cheaper**	
Goose - a 10 lb bird	10s 10d	£25.16p	Frozen 10lb bird £23. Fresh dearer	
Grapes per lb	10d - 2s	£1.94 - £2.13p	Varies. 99p - £2.50p **cheaper**	
Herrings	less than 1d each	less than 18p each	77p average	much dearer now
Leg of lamb per lb	9d - 11d	£1.75 - £2.13p	£2.75p - more if organic dearer now	
Lemons - each	2d	39p	16p	**much cheaper**
Mackerel - each	6d - 8d	£1.16p - £1.55p	£1.1p or cheaper	**cheaper**
Oatmeal per lb	3d	58p	32p	**cheaper**
Onions per lb	a half penny	10p	27p	dearer now
Oranges - each	less than 1d	less than 18p	22p - 40p	dearer now
Pearl Barley - 1 lb	2d - 3d	49p average	£1.77p	much dearer now
Pork per lb	8d	£1. 55p	£1.58 - £3. 62p dearer now	
Port Wine	2s 1d	£4. 84	£4.98 cheapest dearer now	
Raisins per lb	5d	97p	£1. 15p - £2. 18p	dearer now
Rice per lb	3d	58p	40p average. **cheaper**	
Sugar - white	3d - 4d per 1 lb	58p - 72p	49p	**cheaper**
Sugar - brown	2d per lb	39p	66p	dearer now